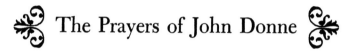 The Prayers of John Donne

THE
PRAYERS
OF
JOHN DONNE

*Selected and Edited from the Earliest
Sources, with an Essay on Donne's
Idea of Prayer*

BY

Herbert H. Umbach, *Ph. D.*

*Professor of English
Valparaiso University*

BOOKMAN ASSOCIATES
NEW YORK

And so as your eyes that stay here, and mine that must be far of[f], for all that distance shall meet every morning, in looking upon that same Sun, and meet every night, in looking upon the same Moon; so our hearts may meet morning and evening in that God, which sees and hears everywhere; that you may come thither to him with your prayers, that I, (if I may be of use for his glory, and your edification in this place) may be restored to you again; and [that I] may come to him with my prayer that what Paul soever plant amongst you, or what Apollos soever water, God himself will give us the increase: That if I never meet you again till we have all passed the gate of death, yet in the gates of heaven, I may meet you all, and there say to my Saviour and your Saviour, that which he said to his Father and our Father, *Of those whom thou hast given me, have I not lost one.*

JOHN DONNE, Peroration of *A Sermon of Valediction at my going into Germany, at Lincoln's-Inne,* April 18, 1619 (*XXVI Sermons,* #19, p. 280)

✣ Preface ✣

A MODERN FOR more than three hundred years, the author of
the various prayers gathered in this book is an eloquent voice
expressing the ceaseless yearning of man's soul for the peace that
passeth understanding. Christian readers will find this a useful
little volume for devotional purposes; in addition, Donne schol-
ars will discover herein an hitherto ungrouped unit of carefully
selected spiritual meditations of the celebrated poet-preacher.

John Donne (1572-1631) lived during significant days in
England. In an historical period which was important not only
for the Authorized or King James Version of the Bible, but also
and especially for its influential manuals of devotion, its numerous directives for public prayer and worship, and the great
Book of Common Prayer itself, it would be natural for a believer
to treasure the universal hope and joy that can be his through
prayer. In these outpourings from Donne's heart there is an ad-
ditional something, a something special in power, grace, and
appropriateness. Indeed this man knew the privilege of prayer!

We should not forget the importance of the fact that the
writer of these devotions had been a layman for more than twice
as long as he was a clergyman. Ordained late in life, in the year
1615, he had by then established his habits of feeling and think-
ing—before he had to compose prayers by virtue of his calling.
This collection presents some prayers also of young Donne.
Moreover, it was an unexpected turn of events that had shaped
the career of this poet and secretary into the professional chan-
nels of the Anglican Church of the early seventeenth century.
Like his beloved St. Augustine, his past life provided a dramatic

contrast to later almost saintly years. With an ability characteristic
of Renaissance man, the Dean of St. Paul's Cathedral in London
put to new use an unmatched literary talent of metaphysical expression and artistic sense of rhythm prominent in his youthful
love poetry. Better than that, he learned to excel (doubtless
by continuous practice and innate prayer aptitude) in communi-
cating the art of prayer.

To help us determine a man's idea of prayer as the key to
his supplications and thanksgivings, more valuable than an out-
line of the religious party or creed to which he belongs is an
analysis of his individual temperament and of the spiritual motivation within him. Neither the establishment of truth nor argu-
mentation about its processes is in place in prayer. Instead, prayer
will grow out of deep personal convictions, from fullness of
realization with the psalmist that *Thou, Lord, art good, and
ready to forgive, and plenteous in mercy unto all them that call
upon Thee.* My introduction, accordingly, presents our author's
concept of prayer, mostly in his very words, as background for
the prayers themselves.

The prayer-life so fervently recorded in the following pages
arises from a "poore intricated soule! Riddling, perplexed, laby-
rinthicall soule" which sincerely strives to rise above its human
level. Because Donne has a way of saying things that strike a
chime in our own memory, throughout it all I sense strongly the
articulate individual rather than the official cleric. *Not as though
I had already attained,* St. Paul's motto, echoes Donne's approach; together with it there is David's corollary, *Blessed is he
whose transgression is forgiven, . . . unto whom the Lord im-
puteth not iniquity, and in whose spirit there is no guile.* That
our Heavenly Father hates sin but will restore the repentant sinner is the Biblical emphasis in all of Donne's prayers and comments on prayer.

A familiar passage written by Shakespeare on the futility of
King Claudius' external motions without sincerity in prayer is
strikingly similar to what his contemporary Donne once said
in a prebend sermon preached at St. Paul's on November 5,

Preface

1626: "To come to God there is a straight line for every man every where: But this we doe not, if we come not with our heart. *Praebe mihi fili cor tuum,* saith God, *My sonne give me thy heart* [margin reference, Proverbs 23, 26]." This edition shows us Donne's heart intimately communing with God himself.

The responsibility for facts and opinions in this book is entirely mine, but credit is due my wife and daughter for encouragement during the entire venture. Especially The Folger Shakespeare Library and The Library of Congress were my workshop. To the President and Board of Directors of Valparaiso University I express gratitude for assistance in publishing this scholarly work. For kind permission to quote and otherwise use copyright material I thank particularly The Clarendon Press, and Random House. Other indebtedness is acknowledged in my Notes.

HERBERT H. UMBACH

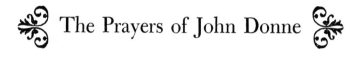 The Prayers of John Donne

 Contents

Introduction

What did Donne say and write *about* religious prayer? His actual prayers are the practice, the result; but what is, so to speak, his theory and idea and concept of prayer? For this basic information we turn to his published remarks and to those of his first biographer concerning this point. Source identification and helps are available in the Notes. For the most part, these are fresh excerpts in as much as no one heretofore has taken time to examine all the numerous comments which Donne made in his observations on the idea of prayer. Notice how modern is his unusual ability in self-analysis for the benefit of other persons, ourselves included.

The duty of prayer, though wee be elsewhere [margin: 1 Thess. 5, 17] commanded *To pray continually,* yet for all that continuall disposition, we have here [in the text of this sermon, Ps. 32, 6] certaine limitations, or rather indeed preparations, lest that which we call Prayer should not be so, and these are foure: For first, it is but *omnis sanctus,* every godly man shall pray, for the prayer of the wicked turns to sinne; And then the object of prayer, to whom it must be directed, is limited, it is but *ad te,* unto thee hee shall pray, beyond him wee cannot goe, and he that prayes short of him, to any on this side of God, falls short in his prayer; And in a third consideration, the subject, the matter of his prayer is limited too, It is but *propter hoc,* for this shall hee pray, that is, for that which hath beene formerly expressed, not whatsoever our desires, or our anguish, and vexation, and impatience presents or suggests to us: And lastly, the time is limited too, *In tempore opportuno,* In a time when thou mayest be found.[1]

Such is the general picture as given by the preacher in the opening paragraph of a powerful sermon on one of the penitential psalms, the prayer-book of the Bible. Human frailty, however, will always handicap him who prays.

But when we consider with a religious seriousnesse the manifold weaknesses of the strongest devotions in time of Prayer, it is a sad consideration. I throw my selfe downe in my Chamber, and I call in, and invite God, and his Angels thither, and when they are there, I neglect God and his Angels, for the noise of a Flie, for the ratling of a Coach, for the whining of a doore; I talk on, in the same posture of praying; Eyes lifted up; knees bowed downe; as though I prayed to God; and, if God, or his Angels should aske me, when I thought last of God in that prayer, I cannot tell: Sometimes I finde that I had forgot what I was about, but when I began to forget it, I cannot tell. A memory of yesterday's pleasures, a feare of to morrow's dangers, a straw under my knee, a noise in mine eare, a light in mine eye, an any thing, a nothing, a fancy, a Chimera in my braine, troubles me in my prayer. So certainely is there nothing, nothing in spirituall things, perfect in this world.[2]

Earlier, in a letter, the lay Donne had indicated this same feeling of personal insufficiency: "Two of the most precious things which God hath afforded us here [in this world], for the agony and exercise of our sense and spirit, which are a thirst and inhiation after the next life, and a frequency of prayer and meditation in this, are often envenomed, and putrefied, and stray into a corrupt disease."[3] In a poem he writes similarly,

> Oh, to vex me, contraryes meet in one:
> Inconstancy unnaturally hath begott
> A constant habit; that when I would not
> I change in vowes, and in devotione.
> As humorous is my contritione

14

As my prophane Love, and as soone forgott:
As ridlingly distemper'd, cold and hott,
As praying, as mute; as infinite, as none.
I durst not view heaven yesterday; and to day
In prayers, and flattering speaches I court God:
To morrow I quake with true feare of his rod.
So my devout fitts come and go away
Like a fantastique Ague: save that here
Those are my best dayes, when I shake with feare.[4]

The dilemma of flesh versus spirit plagued Donne frequently.
"In sudden and unpremeditate prayer, I am not alwayes I; and
when I am not my self, my prayer is not my prayer. Passions and
affections sometimes, sometimes bodily infirmities, and sometimes a vain desire of being eloquent in prayer, alien[ate]s
me, withdraws me from my self, and then that prayer is not
my prayer."[5] Characteristically Donne follows up this point with
an illustration. "Though that prayer which Luther is said to have
said upon his death-bed, *Oremus pro Domino Deo nostro Iesu
Christo,* Let us pray for our Lord and Saviour Christ Jesus, may
admit a good sense, because Christ being (as S[t]. Augustine
sayes often) *Caput et Corpus,* both the Head and the Body, as he
is the Body, the Church, subject to so many pressures, he had
need to be prayed for; yet his [Luther's] state being considered
at that time, almost at the last gasp, he being scarce he, that
prayer can scarce be called his prayer."

Negligence, even after premeditation, is fostered by man's
ceaseless foe, the "prince of darknesse," asserts Donne in another
autobiographic passage that lends vividness to his sermons.

I turne to hearty and earnest prayer to God, and I fix my
thoughts strongly (as I thinke) upon him, and before I have
perfected one petition, one period of my prayer, a power and
principality is got into me againe. *Spiritus soporis* [margin:
Esay 29, 10], The spirit of slumber closes mine eyes, and I pray
drousily; Or *Spiritus vertiginis* [margin: Esay 19, 14], the
spirit of deviation, and vaine repetition, and I pray giddily, and

15

circularly, and returne againe and againe to that I have said before, and perceive not that I do so; and *nescio cujus spiritus sim,* (as our Saviour said, rebuking his Disciples, who were so vehement for the burning of the Samaritans, *you know not of what spirit you are* [margin: Luke 9, 55]) I pray, and know not of what spirit I am, I consider not mine own purpose in prayer; And by this advantage, this doore of inconsideration, enters *spiritus erroris,* The seducing spirit, the spirit of error [margin: 1 Tim. 4, 1], and I pray not onely negligently, but erroniously, dangerously, for such things as disconduce to the glory of God, and my true happinesse, if they were granted. Nay, even the prophet Hosea's *spiritus fornicationum* enters into me, The spirit of fornication, that is, some remembrance of the wantonnesse of my youth, some mis-interpretation of a word in my prayer, that may beare an ill sense, some unclean spirit, some power or principality hath depraved my prayer, and slack'ned my zeale.[6]

With such natural handicaps, the plight of an individual becomes more acute if he be the head of a family and seek to please God with the words of his mouth and the meditations of his heart. "Beloved, since every master of a family, who is a Bishop in his house, should call his family together, to humble, and powre out their soules to God, let him consider, that when he comes to kneele at the side of his table, to pray, he comes to build a Church there; and therefore should sanctifie that place, with a due, and penitent consideration. . . . When thou kneelest down at thy bed side, to shut up the day at night, or to beginne it in the morning, thy servants, thy children, thy little flock about thee, there thou buildest a Church too: And therefore sanctifie that place; wash it with thy tears, and with a repentant consideration."[7]

Faith alone, in harmony with the promise of Jesus, *If thou canst believe, all things are possible to him that believeth,* is the secret of power in prayer. But how can the ordinary human being achieve such power? Especially when abject? Wrestling with this problem, Donne says:

Introduction

... as long as we are in this valley of tentations, there is nothing, no not [even] in spirituall things, not in faith it selfe perfect.

It is not *In credendis* ["in things that we are bound to believe," context], in our embracing the object of faith; we doe not that perfectly; It is not *In petendis* ["in things that we are bound to pray for"], in our directing our prayers faithfully neither; we doe not that; our faith is not perfect, nor our hope is not perfect; for, so argues the Apostle [margin: Iames 4, 3], *Ye aske, and receive not, because ye aske amisse;* you cannot hope constantly, because you doe not pray aright: And to make a Prayer a right Prayer, there go so many essentiall circumstances, as that the best man may justly suspect his best Prayer: for, since Prayer must bee of faith, Prayer can be but so perfect, as the faith is perfect; and the imperfections of the best faith we have seene. Christ hath given us but a short Prayer; and yet we are weary of that. Some of the old Heretiques of the Primitive Church abridged that Prayer, and some of our later Schismatiques have annihilated, evacuated that Prayer: The Cathari then, left out that one Petition, *Dimitte nobis, Forgive us our trespasses,* for they thought themselves so pure, as that they needed no forgivenesse, and our new men leave out the whole Prayer, because the same Spirit that spake in Christ, speakes in their extemporall prayers, and they can pray, as well as Christ could teach them. And . . . which of us ever, ever sayes over that short Prayer, with a deliberate understanding of every Petition as we passe, or without deviations, and extravagancies of our thoughts, in that halfe-minute of our Devotion?[8]

Although Donne maintained a firm stand against slovenly prayer ("You would scarce thanke a man for an extemporall Elegy, or Epigram or Panegyrique in your praise, if it cost the poet, or the orator no paines. God will scarce hearken to sudden inconsidered, irreverent prayers."[9]), he felt certain of gospel forgiveness and comfort for sincere pray-ers in our imperfect world.

There is no forme of Building stronger than an Arch, and yet an Arch hath declinations, which even a flat-roofe hath not; The flat-roofe lies equall in all parts; the Arch declines downwards in all parts, and yet the Arch is a firme supporter. Our Devotions doe not the lesse beare us upright, in the sight of God, because they have declinations towards natural affections: God doth easilier pardon some neglectings of his grace, when it proceeds out of a tendernesse, or may be excused out of good nature, than any presuming upon his grace. If a man doe depart in some actions, from an exact obedience of God's will, upon infirmity, or humane affections, and not a contempt, God passes it over often times. For, when our Saviour Christ sayes, *Be pure as your Father in heaven is pure,* that is a rule for our purity, but not a measure of our purity; It is that we should be pure so, not that we should be so pure as our Father in heaven. When we consider that weaknesse, that went through the Apostles, even to Christ's Ascension, that they looked for a temporall Kingdome, and for preferment in that; when we consider that weaknesse in the chiefe of them, S[t]. Peter, at the Transfiguration, when, as the Text sayes [margin: Mark 9, 6], *He knew not what to say;* when we consider the weaknesse of his action, that for feare of death, he renounced the Lord of Life, and denied his Master; when in this very story [of this sermon's text, John 11, 21], when Christ said that Lazarus was *asleepe,* and that *he would goe to awake him,* they could understand it so impertinently, as that Christ should goe such a journey, to come to the waking of a man, asleep at that time when he spoke; All these infirmities of theirs, multiply this consolation upon us, That though God look upon the Inscription, he looks upon the metall too, Though he look that his Image should be preserved in us, he looks in what earthen vessels this Image is put, and put by his own hand; and though he hate us in our rebellions, yet he pities us in our grievances; though he would have us better, he forsakes us not for every degree of illnesse. There are three great dangers in this consideration of perfectnesse, and purity; First, to distrust of God's mercy, if thou finde not this purity in thy selfe, and this perfectnesse; And then to presume upon God, nay upon thine own right, in an overvaluing of thine own purity, and perfectnesse; And againe, to condemne others, whom thou wilt needs thinke lesse pure, or perfect than thy selfe. Against this diffidence in God, to thinke our selves so desperately impure, as that God will not look upon us; And this presumption in God, to thinke our selves so pure, as that God is bound to look upon us; And this un-

charitablenesse towards others, to think none pure at all, that are
not pure our way; Christ armes us by his Example, He receives
these sisters of Lazarus, and accomplishes as much as they de-
sired, though there were weaknesses in their Faith, in their
Hope, in their Charity, expressed in that unperfect speech, *Lord,
if thou hadst been here, my brother had not dyed*: for, there is
nothing not [even] in spirituall things perfect.[10]

With all of his tolerance, Donne none the less differed in manner from the Puritans of his day. "I would also rather make short
prayers than extend them, though God can neither be surprised,
nor besieged; for, long prayers have more of the man, as ambi-
tion of eloquence, and a complacencie in the work, and more of
the Devil by often distractions: for, after in the beginning we
have well intreated God to hearken, we speak no more to him."[11]
Included among short prayers are those we make subconsciously.

That soule, that is accustomed to direct her selfe to God, upon
every occasion, that, as a flowre at Sun-rising, conceives a sense
of God, in every beame of his, and spreads and dilates it selfe
towards him, in a thankfulnesse, in every small blessing that he
sheds upon her; that soule, that as a flowre at the Sun's declining,
contracts and gathers in, and shuts up her selfe, as though
she had received a blow, when soever she heares her Saviour
wounded by a[n] oath, or blasphemy, or exacration; that soule,
who, whatsoever string be strucken in her, base or treble, her
high or her low estate, is ever tun'd toward God, that soule
prayes sometimes when it does not know that it prayes. I heare
that man name God, and aske him what said you, and perchance
he cannot tell; but I remember, that he casts forth some of those
ejaculationes animae, (as S[t] August[ine]: calls them) some of
those darts of a devout soule, which, though they have not particular deliberations, and be not formall prayers, yet they are the
indicia, pregnant evidences and blessed fruits of a religious custome; much more is it true, which S[t]. Bernard saies there, of
them, *Deus audit,* God heares that voice of the heart, which the
heart it selfe heares not, that is, at first considers not. Those occasionall and transitory prayers, and those fixed and stationary
prayers, for which, many times, we binde our selves to private

prayer at such a time, are payments of this debt, in such peeces, and in such summes, as God, no doubt, accepts at our hands. But yet the solemne dayes of payment, are the Sabbaths of the Lord, and the place of this payment, is the house of the Lord, where, as Tertullian expresses it, *Agmine facto,* we muster our forces together, and besiege God; that is, not taking up every tatter'd fellow, every sudden ragge or fragment of speech, that rises from our tongue, or our affections, but mustering up those words, which the Church hath levied for that service, in the Confessions, and Absolutions, and Collects, and Litanies of the Church, we pay this debt, and we receive our acquittance.[12]

Even the standardized phrases of the liturgy or of the psalms or—as in the quotation following—of the creed, however, will not guarantee the complete attentiveness which God deserves when we pray in private. As each churchgoer knows richly, the influence of public prayer is more beneficial for easing the broken heart and the contrite spirit.

If I get farther than this [*"Credo Ecclesiam Catholicam, I beleeve the holy Catholique Church"*] in the Creed, to the *Credo in Spiritum Sanctum, I beleeve in the Holy Ghost,* where shall I finde the Holy Ghost? I lock my doore to my selfe, and I throw my selfe downe in the presence of my God, I devest my selfe of all worldly thoughts, and I bend all my powers, and faculties upon God, as I think, and suddenly I finde my selfe scattered, melted, fallen into vaine thoughts, into no thoughts; I am upon my knees, and I talke, and think nothing; I deprehend my selfe in it, and I goe about to mend it, I gather new forces, new purposes to try againe, and doe better, and I doe the same thing againe. *I beleeve in the Holy Ghost,* but doe not finde him, if I seeke him onely in private prayer; But in *Ecclesia,* when I goe to meet him in the *Church,* when I seeke him where hee hath promised to be found . . . instantly the savour of this Myrrhe is exalted, and multiplied to me; not a dew, but a shower is powred out upon me, and presently followes *Communio Sanctorum, The Communion of Saints,* the assistance of Militant and Triumphant Church in my behalfe.[13]

Introduction

Advantages of the time and place which group prayer activity can give an individual would naturally furnish a preacher with persuasive material. Donne combines all of his varied resources in discussing this topic. Notice the clarity of logic, echoing the sometime law student, in the next passage.

When we say, that God is not tied to places, we must not meane, but that God is otherwise present, and workes otherwise, in places consecrated to his service, than in every prophane place. When I pray in my chamber, I build a Temple there, that houre; And, that minute, when I cast out a prayer, in the street, I build a Temple there; And when my soule prayes without any voyce, my very body is then a Temple: And God, who knowes what I am doing in these actions, erecting these Temples, he comes to them, and prospers, and blesses my devotions; and shall not I come to his Temple, where he is alwaies resident? My chamber were no Temple, my body were no Temple, except God came to it; but whether I come hither, or no, this [church] will be God's Temple: I may lose by my absence; He gaines nothing by my comming. He that hath a cause to be heard, will not goe to Smithfield, nor he that hath cattaile to buy or sell, to Westminster; He that hath bargaines to make, or newes to tell, should not come to doe that at Church; nor he that hath prayers to make, walke in the fields for his devotions. If I have a great friend, though in cases of necessity, as sicknesse, or other restraints, hee will vouchsafe to visit me, yet I must make my suits to him at home, at his owne house. In cases of necessity, Christ in the Sacrament, vouchsafes to come home to me; And the Court is where the King is; his blessings are with his Ordinances, wheresoever: But the place to which he hath invited me, is his house. Hee that made the great Supper in the Gospel, called in new guests; but he sent out no meat to them, who had been invited, and might have come, and came not. Chamber-prayers, single, or with your family, Chamber-Sermons, Sermons read over there; and Chamber-Sacraments, administered in necessity there, are blessed assistants, and supplements; they are as the almes at the gate, but the feast is within; they are as a cock of water without, but the Cistern is within; *habenti dabitur;* he that hath a handfull of devotion at home, shall have his devotion multiplyed to a Gomer here; for when he is become a part of the Congregation, he is joynt-tenant with them, and the devotion of all the Congregation, and the blessings upon all the Congregation, are his blessings, and his devotions.[14]

By fellowship of communal prayer in church whenever possible, the individual can better hope for and experience in unison the concentration upon serious matters that he sorely lacks at home. "Here in the Congregation we cannot suck in a word from the preacher, we cannot speak, we cannot sigh a prayer to God, but that that whole breath and aire is made of mercy."[15] I consider this a significant commentary upon Isaiah's inspired words (56, 7): *Mine house shall be called an house of prayer for all people.* Again listen to Donne the officiant as he says:

I bring not a Star-chamber with me up into the Pulpit, to punish a forgery, if you counterfeit a zeale in coming hither now; nor an Exchequer, to punish usurious contracts, though made in the Church; nor a high Commission, to punish incontinencies, if they be promoted by wanton interchange of looks, in this place. Onely by my prayers, which he hath promised to accompany and prosper in his service, I can diffuse his overshadowing Spirit over all the corners of this Congregation, and pray that Publican, that stands below afar off, and dares not lift up his eyes to heaven, to receive a chearfull confidence, that his sinnes are forgiven him; and pray that Pharisee, that stands above, and onely thanks God, that he is not like other men, to believe himself to be, if not a rebellious, yet an unprofitable servant. I can onely tell them, that neither of them is in the right way of reconciliation to God, *Nec qui impugnant gratiam, nec qui superbè gratias agunt,* neither he who by a diffidence hinders the working of God's grace, nor he that thanks God in such a fashion, as though all that he had received, were not of meer mercy, but between a debt and a benefit, and that he had either merited before, or paid God after, in pious works, for all, and for more than he hath received at God's hand.[16]

This strong note of warning against spiritual indifference as an external sign of weakness of faith also in church, when we permit competing worldly interests to dominate us, rouses Donne's holy ire to feverish intensity.

Betweene these two [illustrations which Donne had taken from St. Augustine], this licencious comming, and this treacherous comming, there are many commings to Church, commings for company, for observation, for musique: And all these indispositions are ill at prayers; there they are unwholesome, but at the Sacrament, deadly: He that brings any collaterall respect to prayers, looses the benefit of the prayers of the Congregation; and he that brings that to a Sermon, looses the blessing of God's ordinance in that Sermon; hee heares but the Logique, or the Retorique, or the Ethique, or the poetry of the Sermon, but the Sermon of the Sermon he heares not; but he that brings this disposition to the Sacrament, ends not in the losse of a benefit, but he acquires, and procures his owne damnation.[17]

Closely associated with this conviction is a brief revelation of his personal practice recorded near the ending of *A Hymne to Christ*:

> Seale then this bill of my Divorce to All,
> On whom those fainter beames of love did fall;
> Marry those loves, which in youth scattered bee
> On Fame, Wit, Hopes (false mistresses) to thee.
> Churches are best for Prayer, that have least light:
> To see God only, I goe out of sight.[18]

Inevitably aware of such human inadequacies in so important an act of worship, Donne takes courage from the cardinal essential of Christian prayer, namely that it be made in the name and through the vicarious virtue of Jesus Christ. "As therefore the Church of God scarce presents any petition, any prayer to God, but it is subscribed by Christ; the Name of Christ, is for the most part the end, and the seale of all our Collects; all our prayers in the Liturgy, (though they be but for temporall things, for Plenty, or Peace, or Faire-weather) are shut up so, *Grant this O*

Lord, for our Lord and Saviour Christ Iesus' sake: So David for
our example, drives all his petitions in this Text [Psalm 6, 4 and
5], to this Conclusion, *Salvum me fac, O Lord save me;* that is,
apply that salvation, Christ Jesus to me."[19] "For even of a devout
use of that very name, do some of the Fathers interpret that,
Oleŭ[m] effusum Nomen tuii, That the name of Iesus should
be spread as an ointment, breathed as perfume, diffused as a soul
over all the petitions of our prayers; As the Church concludes for
the most part, all her Collects so, *Grant this O Lord, for our
Lord and Saviour Christ Iesus' sake.*"[20]

In private or in public, certainly prayer should find words for
its expression. Forms of speech, whispered or audible, are generally needed to sustain the mind in this supreme exertion. Donne feels certain that God Himself will aid the struggling individual, even as does a prince his subject.

Though therefore some extreme contemplative philosophers
have thought itt to be the highest degree of reverence which man
could use towards God to abstaine from outward sacrifices and
from verball prayer, because nothinge but our purest thoughts,
before they are mingled with any affections or passions, can have
any proportion to God or gett within any distance of him, yett
they err'd, because they thought we went to God in these actions
when indeed God comes to us. So also do princes descend to receive the offices of such men as cannot reach up to them; for
therefore hath God allowed them so many of his own attributes,
that they might not take a measure of their greatnes by the low-
nes of others but by their conforminge themselves to him and
doinge as he doth. And therefore though I might have performed some part of my duty by continuinge in my private prayers
in my study for your Highnes [The Prince of Wales] and this
state, yett I cannot fear but that you will also descend to this
[letter] and accept the same duty as it is thus uttered and ap-
parelled in this booke [*Pseudo-Martyr*].[21]

But suppose that the devil and our sinful flesh make us doubt
the genuineness of our prayers to God, and make us despair of

Introduction

God's listening to us. What then? "If thou pray, and hast an apprehension that thou hearest God say, hee will not heare thy prayers, doe not beleeve that it is hee that speakes; If thou canst not chuse but beleeve that it is he, let mee say, in a pious sense, doe not beleeve him: God would not bee beleeved, in denouncing of Iudgements, so absolutely, so peremptorily, as to bee thought to speake unconditionally, illimitedly: God tooke it well at David's hands, that when the Prophet had tolde him, *The childe shall surely die,* yet hee beleeved not the Prophet so peremptorily, but that hee proceeded in Prayer to God, for the life of the childe. Say with David [margin: Psalm 61, 4; 62, 7], *Thou hast beene a strong Tower to mee; I will abide in thy Tabernacle, Et non Emigrabo,* I will never goe out."[22]

God is indeed, as Scripture says, *a spirit; and they that worship Him must worship Him in spirit and in truth.* Donne correctly concludes that this supernatural quality does not mean, however, that we are to think of our Heavenly Father as other than an accessible God to whom we are to pray personally, frequently, fervently, and specifically.

I must not wrap up all my necessities in generall termes in my prayers, but descend to particulars; For this places my devotion upon particular considerations of God, to consider him in every Attribute, what God hath done for me in Power, what in Wisedome, what in Mercy; which is a great assistance, and establishing, and propagation of devotion. As it is a degree of unthankfulnesse, to thank God too generally, and not to delight to insist upon the waight, and measure, and proportion, and the goodnesse of every particular mercy: so is it an irreverent, and inconsiderate thing, not to take my particular wants into my thoughts, and into my prayers, that so I may take a holy knowledge, that I have nothing, nothing but from God, and by prayer. And as God is an accessible God, as he is his owne Master of Requests, and is ever open to receive thy Pe[ti]tions, in how small a matter soever: so is he an inexhaustible God, he can give infinitely, and an indefatigable God, he cannot be pressed too much. Therefore hath Christ given us a Parable [margin: Luke 11, 5 and 18, 7] of getting Bread at midnight by Importunity, and not otherwise; And another of a Iudge that heard the widow's cause by Importunity, and not otherwise; And, not a Parable, but a History, and a History of his own [margin: Matt. 15, 21], of a woman of Canaan, that overcame him in the behalfe of her daughter, by Importunity; when, but by importunity, she could not get so much as an answer, as a deniall at his hands. Pray personally, rely not upon dead nor living Saints; Thy Mother the Church prayes for thee, but pray for thy selfe too. . . . Pray personally, and pray frequently; David had ma[n]y stationary times of the day, and night too, to pray in. Pray frequently, and pray fervently; God took it not ill, at David's hands, to be awaked, and to be called up, as though hee were asleepe at our prayers, and to be called upon, to pull his hand out of his bosome, as though he were slack in relieving our necessities. This was a weaknesse in those Sisters [of Lazarus, i.e. Mary and Martha], that they solicited not Christ in person; still get as neare God as you can; And that they declared not their case particularly; It is not enough to pray, nor to confesse in general termes; And, that they pursued not their prayer earnestly, thorowly; It is not enough to have prayed once; Christ does not onely excuse, but enjoine Importunity. [23]

This reiteration of importunity in prayer is, it seems to me, our very best clue to Donne's own prayer technique; it likewise indicates the source of his strength. Observe his psychology of prayer in another passage. "It may be mentall, for we may thinke prayers. It may be vocall, for we may speake prayers. It may be actuall, for we do prayers. . . . So then to do the office of your vocation sincerely, is to pray. . . . In the sinfull consumption of the soule, a stupidity and indisposition to prayer must first be cured. . . . Things absolutely good, [such] as Remission of sinnes, we may absolutely beg: and, to escape things absolutely ill, [such] as sinne. But mean and indifferent things, qualified by the circumstances, we must aske conditionally and referringly to the giver's will."[24]

Prayer is our whole service to God. Earnest Prayer hath the

nature of Importunity; Wee presse, wee importune God in Prayer; Yet that puts not God to a morosity, to a frowardnesse; God flings not away from that; God suffers that importunity, and more. Prayer hath the nature of Impudency; Wee threaten God in Prayer; as Gregor[y] : Nazi[anzen] : adventures to expresse it; He saies, his Sister, in the vehemence of her Prayer, would threaten God, *Et honesta quadam impudentia, egit impudentem;* She came, saies he, to a religious impudency with God, and to threaten him, that she would never depart from his Altar, till she had her Petition granted; And God suffers this Impudency, and more. Prayer hath the nature of Violence; In the publique Prayers of the Congregation, we besiege God, saies Tertul[lian] : and we take God Prisoner, and bring God to our Conditions; and God is glad to be strait'ned by us in that siege. This Prophet here [in this sermon's text, Psalm 6, 4 and 5] executes before, what the Apostle counsailes after, *Pray incessantly;* Even in his singing he prayes; And as St. Basil saies, *Etiam somnia justorum preces sunt,* A Good man's dreames are Prayers, he prayes, and not sleepily, in his sleepe, so David's Songs are Prayers.[25]

A beautiful, short summary of prayer motivation is this comprehensive assertion by Donne: "He [God] loves to hear us tell him, even those things which he knew before; his Benefits in our Thankfulness, And our sins in our Confessions, And our necessities in our Petitions."[26] His first biographer—who had been one of his parishioners, Izaak Walton,—tells us that Donne practised what he preached. For instance, "He [Donne] did much contemplate (especially after he ent'red into his Sacred Calling) the mercies of Almighty God, the immortality of the Soul, and the joyes of Heaven; and would often say, Blessed be God that he is God divinely like himself."[27] Or, again, "He blest each yeare's poore remainder with a thankfull Prayer,"[28] as found in the private account book kept after his entrance into his deanery (see Group 6 A).

In an interesting doctrinal sermon Donne discusses "the Ten Commandements, which is the sum of all that we are to doe; The Lord's Prayer, which is the summe of all that we are to ask;

and the Apostles' Creed, which is the summe of all that wee are to beleeve."[29] Important for our analysis here is a lengthy passage on the Lord's Prayer, from similar contexts, with emphasis upon the integral relationship of prayer and praise.

Such is the constitution and frame of that Prayer of Prayers, That which is the extraction of all prayers, and draws into a summe all that is in all others, That which is the infusion into all others, sheds and showres whatsoever is acceptable to God, in any other prayer, That Prayer which our Saviour gave us, (for as he meant to give us all for asking, so he meant to give us the words by which we should ask) As that Prayer consists of seven petitions, and seven is infinite, so by being at first begun with glory and acknowledgement of his raigning in heaven, and then shut up in the same manner, with acclamations of power and glory, it is made a circle of praise, and a circle is infinite too, The Prayer, and the Praise is equally infinite. Infinitely poore and needy man, that ever needst infinite things to pray for; Infinitely rich and abundant man, that ever hast infinite blessings to praise God for.

God's house in this world is called the house of Prayer; but in heaven it is the house of Praise: No surprisall with any new necessities there, but one even, incessant, and everlasting tenor of thanksgiving; And it is a blessed inchoation of that state here, here to be continually exercised in the commemoration of God's former goodnesse towards us. . . .

If we compare these two incomparable duties, Prayer and Praise, it will stand thus, Our Prayers besiege God, (as Tertullian speakes, especially of publique Prayer in the Congregation, *Agmine facto obsidemus Deum*) but our praises prescribe in God, we urge him, and presse him with his ancient mercies, his mercies of old: By Prayer we incline him, we bend him, but by Praise we bind him; our thanks for former benefits, is a producing of a specialty, by which he hath contracted with us for more. In Prayer we sue to him, but in our Praise we sue him himselfe; Prayer is as our petition, but Praise is as our Evidence; In that we beg, in this we plead. God hath no law upon himselfe, but yet God himselfe proceeds by precedent: And whensoever we present to him with thanksgiving, what he hath done, he does the same, and more againe. Neither certainly can the Church institute any prayers, more effectuall for the preservation of Religion, or of the State, than the Collects for our deliverances, in the like cases before: And when he heares them, though they have the nature of Praise onely, yet he translates them into Prayers, and when we our selves know not, how much we stand in need of new deliverances, he delivers us from dangers which we never suspected, from Armies and Navies which we never knew were prepared, and from plots and machinations which we never knew were brought into Consultation, and diverts their forces, and dissipates their counsels with an untimely abortion. . . . prayer consists as much of praise for the past, as of supplication for the future.[30]

Donne provides incidental light on a contemporary anxiety when, as in the previous prayer-praise blending, he illustrates his point. "We say sometimes in scorn to a man, God help you, and God send you wit; and therein, though it have the sound of a prayer, wee call him foole. So wee have seen of late, some in obscure Conventicles, institute certain prayers, That God would keep the King, and the Prince [namely, James I and Charles, respectively] in the true Religion; The prayer is always good, always usefull; but when that prayer is accompanied with circumstances, as though the King and the Prince were declining from that [Anglican] Religion, then even the prayer it selfe is libellous, and seditious; Saint Paul, in that former place, apparels a Subject's prayers well, when hee sayes, *Let prayers bee given with thanks;* Let our prayers bee for continuance of the blessings, which wee have, and let our acknowledgement of present blessings, bee an inducement for future: pray, and praise together; pray thankfully, pray not suspiciously."[31]

His own experience, quoted by Walton, brought Donne the transcendent joy that results from bringing to God prayer and praise: "The words of this Hymne [*A Hymne to God the Father*] have restored to me the same thoughts of joy that possest my soul in my sickness when I composed it. And, O, the

29

power of Church-musick! that harmony added to it has raised the
Affections of my heart, and quic'ned my graces of zeal and gratitude; and I observe, that I always return from paying this pub-
lick duty of Prayer and Praise to God, with an unexpressible
tranquillity of mind, and a willingness to leave the world."[32]
The ending of a letter—addressed To the right honourable the
Countess of Montgomery—expresses the idea this way: ". . . in
thankfulnesse I shall lift up my hands as clean as my infirmities
can keep them, and a voyce as clear as his spirit shall be pleased
to tune in my prayers in all places of the world, which shall
either sustain or bury/Your Ladiship's humble servant in Christ
Iesus."[33]

This hopeful outlook is consistent in Donne because "if our
thoughts bee knowne, much more our actions; If our sighes,
and groanes bee knowne much more our prayers, our confessions,
our [conferences and] devotions, our more manifest, and evident
wayes of seeking, and establishing our reconciliation with
God."[34] As Donne wrote in a verse-letter To the Countesse of
Bedford,

> In none but us [humans], are such mixt engines found,
> As hands of double office: For, the ground
> We till with them; and them to heav'n wee raise;
> Who prayer-lesse labours, or, without this, prayes,
> Doth but one halfe, that's none; He which said, *Plough
> And looke not back,* to looke up doth allow.[35]

And even if God delays response to our prayer, the believer
should retain hope by remembering the example of others who
learned patience in awaiting God's right time.

St. Paul pray'd, and pray'd thrice. . . . Thus St. Paul praied
long for one thing and had another. Abraham prayed and seem'd
to have all he asked, and yet had nothing. . . . Limit not God
therfore in his waies or times, but if you would bee heard by
him, heare him; if you would have him grant your praiers doe

his will. . . . Soe if your owne prayers for your deliverance in any temporall, or spirituall affliction bee not presentlie heard, persever for your selves, as the Churches, and the head of them persevers in your behalfe, and God will certainly deliver you in his tyme, and strengthen you to fight out his battell all the way.[36]

"No prayer of ours, howsoever made in the best disposition, in the best testimony of a rectified conscience, must limit God his time, or appoint him, in what morning, or what houre in the morning, God shall come to our deliverance."[37]

What Donne says about fixed times for praying bears repeating here. As always, the comments harmonize with the Bible; in this particular topic, his remarks show also here the sincerity of his youthful conversion to the doctrines of Protestantism. "Our accesses to his [God's] presence are but his descents into us; and when we get any thing by prayer, he gave us before hand the thing and the petition. For, I scarce think any ineffectuall prayer free from both sin, and the punishment of sin: yet as God seposed a seventh of our time for his exterior worship, and as his Christian Church early presented him a type of the whole year in a Lent, and after imposed the obligation of canonique hours, constituting thereby morall Sabbaths every day; I am farre from dehorting those fixed devotions." What I like is the next sentence in this letter to Sir Henry Goodyer: "But I had rather it were bestowed upon thanksgiving than petition, upon praise than prayer; not that God is indeared by that, or wearied by this; all is one in the receiver, but not in the sender: and thanks doth both offices; for, nothing doth so innocently provoke new graces, as gratitude."[38]

The comfort of being presented to God as innocent as Adam, then when God breathed a soule into him, yea as innocent as Christ Jesus himselfe, when he breathed out his soule to God; oh how blessed is that soule that enjoyes it, and how bold that tongue that goes about to expresse it! This is the blessednesse which the godly attaine to by prayer, but not by every sudden

Lord, Lord, or every occasionall holy interjection, but by serious prayer, invested, as with the former, so with that other circumstance that remains, *In tempore opportuno,* In a time when thou mayest be found.

This time is not those *Horae stativae, Horae canonicae,* those fixed houres in the Romane [Catholic] Church, where men are bound to certaine prayers at certaine houres. Not that it is inconvenient for men to binde themselves to certaine fixed times of prayer in their private Exercises; and though not by such a vow, as that it shall be an impiety, yet by so solemne a purpose, as that it shall be a levity to breake it. I have known the greatest Christian Prince, (in style and Title) [probably Henry IV of France, *Roi tres chretien;* Donne had been in Paris in 1612 with Sir Robert Drury] even at the Audience of an Ambassador, at the sound of a Bell, kneele downe in our presence and pray; and God forbid, he should be blamed for doing so; But to place a merit in observing those times, as they doe, is not a right understanding of this time of finding [God]. Nor is it those transitory and interlocutory prayers, which out of custome and fashion we make, and still proceed in our sin; when we pretend to speake to God, but like Comedians upon a stage, turne over our shoulder, and whisper to the Devill.[39]

Exactly what Donne has in mind by this indictment of misuse of prayer can be determined by his even stronger, more outspoken words in another sermon.

We have not leasure to speake of the abuse of prayer in the Roman Church; where they will antidate [antedate] and postdate their prayers; Say to morrow's prayers to day, and to daye's prayers to morrow, if they have other uses and employments of the due time betweene; where they will trade, and make merchandise of prayers by way of exchange, My man shall fast for me, and I will pray for my man; or my Atturney, and Proxy shall pray for us both, at my charge; nay, where they will play for prayers, and the loser must pray for both; To this there belongs but a holy scorne, and I would faine passe it over quickly.[40]

No indecision here, as during a strategic period in his youth when "he was now ent'red into the nineteenth yeare of his age, and being unresolved in his Religion, . . . he began to survey the body of Divinity, controverted between the Reformed and Roman Church. And [margin: Preface to *Pseudo-Martyr*] as God's blessed Spirit did then awaken him to the search, and in that industry did never forsake him, (they be his owne words) So he calls the same Spirit to witness to his Protestation, that in that search and disquisition he proceeded with humility and diffidence in himselfe, by the safest way of frequent Prayers, and indifferent affection to both parties."[41]

The phrase "by the safest way of frequent prayers" is, in my opinion, a reliable index to both Jack Donne and Dean Donne. A young manhood sadly misspent could not readily produce that spiritual quality of which this book bears record. True, his total experience matured him likewise in this manner; essentially, however, Donne's prayer ability and aptitude were lifelong! Then, when both his ministerial career and life's autumn gave him unbounded occasion for prayer, he could write on January 7th., 1630, in a letter to a familiar friend (there being a general report that Donne was dead) :

This advantage you and my other friends have by my frequent feavers, thåt I am so much the oft'ner at the gates of heaven; And this advantage by the solitude and close imprisonment that they reduce me to after, that I am so much the oft'ner at my Prayers, in which I shall never leave out your happinesse; And I doubt not but amongst his other blessings, God will adde some one [blessing] to you for my Prayers.[42]

And again, "We dispute whether the dead shall pray for the living: and because my life may be short, I pray with the most earnestnesse for you now. By the advantage of sicknesse, I return the oft'ner to that holy exercise."[43] That little word *oftener* betokens a comparative degree with rich implications.

Numerous letters of Donne have this tone, echoed at various stages of his life: "I receive you therefore into my prayers, with

mine own weary soul, and commend my self to yours."[44] And
that this is not a merely polite mannerism, the context readily
reveals. Thus, for instance, a Latin poem-letter and its translation,
—To Mr. George Herbert, with one of my seals, of the Anchor
and Christ,—includes this sentiment:

> Under that little Seal great gifts I send,
> Wishes, and prayers, pawns, and fruits of a friend.[45]

Although Donne could say with pride, "I have quieted the
consciences of many that groaned under the burthen of a wounded spirit, whose Prayers I hope are availeable for me,"[46] he
insisted:

I must not rely upon the prayers of others; not of Angels;
Though they be Ministeriall spirits, and not onely to God himselfe, but between God and man, and so, as they present our
prayers, no doubt poure out their owne for us too, yet we
must not rely upon the prayers of Angels. Nor of Saints; Though
they have a more personall, and experimentall sense of our
miseries than Angels have, we must not relie upon the prayers of
Saints. No, nor upon the prayers of the Congregation, though
we see, and heare them pray, except we make our selves parts of
the Congregation, by true devotion, as well as by personall
presence.
It must be mine own prayer, and no prayer is so truly, or so
properly mine, as that that the Church hath delivered and recom-
mended to me.[47]

Among such formal prayers are those for the dead. "In the Primitive Church, when amongst the Fathers there were so divers
opinions of the state of the soul, presently [instantly] after this
life, they easily inclined to be content to do as much for them
dead as when they were alive, and so concurred in a charitable
disposition to pray for them; which manner of prayer then in
use, no Christian Church at this day having received better light,
[we] will allow of."[48] None the less,
. . . a charitable interpretation it becomes us to give of those

prayers for the dead, which we finde in the ancient Fathers; In
S[t]. Augustine for his mother Monica, in S[t]. Ambrose for
his Master Theodosius; They prayed inconsiderately, and upon
consideration they retracted their prayers; at least, gave such
Expositions of them, as that then they were no prayers, but vehement, and indeed, exorbitant declarations of piety mixt with passion. And so beloved, behooves it thee to do in thine own
behalf, if at any time having cast thy self into the posture of
prayer, upon thy knees, and ent'red into thy prayer thou have
found thy self withdrawn, transported, strayed into some deviations, and by-thoughts; Thou must not think all that devotion
lost; much lesse, that prayer to be turned into sin; for, God, who
hath put all thy tears into his Bottle, all thy words into his Regis-
ter, all thy sighs into his bosome, will also spread that zeale with
which thou ent'redst into thy prayer, over thy whole prayer, and
where that (thine own zeale) is too short, Christ Jesus himself will spread his prayer over thine, and say, Give him, O
Father, that which he hath asked faithfully in my name, and,
where he hath fallen into any deviations or negligences, Father
forgive him, though he knew not what he said.[49]

"The Church of God ever delighted herselfe in a holy officious-
nesse in the Commemoration of Martyrs: . . . And for that, they
came soon to institute and appoynt certaine Liturgies, certaine
Offices (as they called them) certaine Services in the Church,
which should have reference to that, to the Commemoration of
Martyrs; as we have in our Booke of Common Prayer, certaine
Services for Marriage, for Buriall, and for such other holy Cele-
brations."[50] Fixed forms rather than free prayers will be useful
here.

Moreover, says Donne, the essential of true prayer—that it be
to the Triune God, and not to man—cannot be overemphasized.
Inimitable indeed is his style!

We must be sure to pray, where we may be sure to speed,
and onely God can give. It is a strange thing, saies Iustin Martyr,
to pray to Esculapius or to Apollo for health, as Gods thereof,
Qui apud Chironem medicinā[m] didicerunt; when they who

pray to them, may know, to whom those gods were beholden for all their medicines, and of whom they learnt all their physick: why should they not rather pray to their Masters, than to them? why should Apollo, Chiroe's scholar, and not Chiro, Apollo's Master, be the god of physick? why should I pray to S[t]. George for victory, when I may goe to the Lord of Hosts, Almighty God himselfe; or consult with a Seargeant, or Corporall, when I may goe to the Generall? Or to another Saint for peace, when I may goe to the Prince of peace Christ Jesus? Why should I pray to Saint Nicolas for a faire passage at Sea, when he that rebuked the storme, is nearer me than S[t]. Nicolas? why should I pray to S[t]. Antony for my hoggs, when he that gave the devill leave to drowne the Gergesens' whole heard [herd] of hoggs, did not doe that by S[t]. Antonie's leave, nor by putting a *caveat* or *prae-non-obstante* in his monopoly of preserving hoggs? I know not where to finde S[t]. Petronilla when I have an ague, nor S[t]. Apollonia, when I have the tooth-ache, nor S[t]. Liberius, when I have the stone: I know not whether they can heare me in Heaven, or no; Our Adversaries will not say, that all Saints in Heaven heare all that is said on earth: I know not whether they be in Heaven, or no: our Adversaries will not say, that the Pope may not erre, in a matter of fact, and so may canonize a Traytor for a Saint: I know not whether those Saints were ever upon earth or no; our Adversaries will not say, that all their Legends were really, historically true, but that many of them, are holy, but yet symbolicall inventions, to figure out not what was truly done before, but what wee should endeavour to doe now. I know my Redeemer liveth, and I know where he is; and no man knowes, where he is not. He is our Creditor, to him we must pray.[51]

Challenging, stimulating, instructive are the many statements of Donne on the idea of prayer. Himself restless until he found rest in God, Donne inevitably encourages us to seek the same source of strength; if not from love, then from duty.

This onely is charity, to doe all, all that we can. And something there is which every man may doe; There are Armies, in the levying whereof, every man is an absolute Prince, and needs no Commission, there are Forces, in which every man is his owne

Muster-master, The force which we spoke of before, out of
Tertullian, the force of prayer; In publique actions, we obey God,
when we obey them to whom God hath committed the publique;
In those things which are in our own power, the subsidies and
contributions of prayer, God looks that we should second his
Faciamus, with our *Dicamus,* That since he must doe all, we
would pray him that he would doe it, And his *Descendamus,*
with our *Ascendamus,* That if we would have him come down,
and fight our battayls, or remove our calamities, we should first
goe up to him, in humble and fervent prayer, That he would
continue the Gospell where it is, and restore it where it was, and
transfer it where it was never as yet heard; Charity is to doe all
to all, and the poorest of us all can doe this to any.[52]

"This is a circumstance, nay, an essentiall difference peculiar to
our debts to God, that we doe not pay them, except we contract
more; we grow best out of debt, by growing farther in debt; by
praying for more, we pay our former debt. *Domus mea Domus
Orationis,* my house, saies God, is a house of prayer; for this use,
and purpose, he built himselfe a house upon earth; He had praise
and glory in heaven before, but for Prayer erected a house here,
his Church. All the world is his Exchequer, he gives in all; from
every creature, from Heaven, and Sea, and Land, and all the in-
habitants of all them, we receive benefits; But the Church is his
Court of Requests, there he receives our petitions, there we receive his answers."[53]

One criticism voiced by Donne against some clergymen of
his day will reveal the depth of his conviction that the prayer
of a sincere person is of great value, even as James wrote (5, 16)
about *effectual fervent prayer.* From Mitcham a letter includes
"my ordinary complaint, That the Divines of these times, are
become meer Advocates, as though Religion were a temporall
inheritance . . . yet that for which they plead is none of theirs.
They write for Religion, without it." After some details comes
this meaningful remark: "we at our lay Altars (which are our
tables, or bedside, or stools, wheresoever we dare prostrate our
selves to God in prayer) must beg it of him,"[54] namely, unity of

faith. Such unity comes only, says Donne repeatedly, when we
"leave all in God's hands, from whose hands nothing can be
wrung by whining but by praying, nor by praying without the
Fiat voluntas tua."⁵⁵ Accordingly, observe in the several next
passages how sincerely Donne shows his Christian understanding of I John 5, 14: *This is the confidence that we have in Him
that, if we ask anything according to His will, He heareth us.*

"Howsoever worldly men engrosse the thanks of the world to
themselves, Christ cast all the honour of all the benefits that he
bestowed upon others, upon his Father; and in his *Veruntamen,*
(*Yet not my will, but thine O Father be done*) He humbled
himselfe, as low as David in his *Non nobis Domine, Not unto
us, O Lord, not unto us, but unto thy Name be all glory
given.*"⁵⁶ Certainly no better example of obedience to God's will
can be found than Christ, so Donne of course speaks of Him
with reverence as the Man of Prayer.

Hee in the daies of his flesh offer'd up prayers, and supplications with strong cryings and teares unto him that was able to
save him from death [margin: Heb. 5, 7]; and was also heard
in that which hee feared, Hee was heard, but when? first, when
pray'd hee that vehement prayer? All agree that that place of the
Apostle hath relation to Christ's praier in his agonie in the garden, *Quando non contentus lachrymis oculorum, totius Corporis
sanguineis lachrimis lachrimavit* [margin: Ambrose], when hee
besides his teares of water opened as many eies as hee had pores
in his body, and wept out blood at every one of those eyes. And
they agree too that that place of the Apostle hath relation to his
vehement prayer upon the crosse, *Eli, Eli, My God, My God,* etc.
. . . So that Christ prayed in his affliction, and yet prayed againe,
That w[hi]ch was David's case [in this sermon's text, Psalm
38, 9], and is ours was his case too, hee was heard, but not at
his first praying; After his first praier of *Transeat calix* hee was
put to his Expostulation, *Quare dereliquisti?* The Father was
allwayes with him; and is with us, but our deliverance is in his
time, and not in ours.⁵⁷

In this spirit of submission the lay Donne wrote from Drury

Introduction

House in 1607—To the gallant Knight, Sir Tho. Lucy—"God loves your soul, if he be loth to let it go inch-meale, and not by swallowings; and he loves it too, if he build it up again stone after stone; his will is not done except his way, and his leasure be observed. . . . the rest of this, I shall make up in my prayers to our blessed Saviour, for all happinesses to you."[58] Later, from him as pastoral friend and counsellor, such comfort carried great meaning; e. g. when Lady Kingsmel's husband had died in 1624:

Then is the will of God done in Earth, as it is in Heaven, when we neither pretermit his actions, nor resist them; neither pass them over in an inconsideration, as though God had no hand in them, nor go about to take them out of his hands, as though we could direct him to do them better. As God's Scriptures are his will, so his actions are his will; both are Testaments, because they testifie his minde to us. It is not lawfull to adde a scedule to either of his wills.[59]

Similarly to Mrs. Cokain in 1629, when a son of hers had died:

But, above all, comfort your self in this, That it is the declared will of God. In sicknesses, and other worldlie crosses, there are anxieties, and perplexities; we wish one thing to day, in the behalf of a distressed child or friend, and another to morrow; because God hath not yet declared his will. But when he hath done that, in death, there is no room for anie anxiety, for anie perplexitie, no, not for a wish; for we may not so much as pray for the dead. You know, David made his child's Sicknesse his Lent, but his Death his Easter: he fasted till the Child's death, but then he returned to his repast, because then he had a declaration of God's will. . . . And, that his pleasure may be either to lessen your crosses, or multiply your strength, shall be the prayer of / Your Brother, and Friend, and / Servant, and Chaplain, / John Donne.[60]

That Donne himself practiced what he advised, we see from a comment like this one in 1628: " . . . my daily Praiers for them all [the members of Mrs. Cokain's family], shall also meet them all. And that's the onely service which I can promise my self an ability to do to God's Church now, since this infirmity in my mouth and voice, is likelie to take me from any frequent exercise of my other duty of Preaching. But, God will either enable me, or pardon me. His will be done upon us all, as his goodnesse hath been overflowingly poured out upon / Your poor Friend, and lovingest / Brother and Servant."[61] Worth mentioning, too, is this characteristic assertion in a sermon preached at Lincoln's Inn: "At the day of our death, we write *Pridie resurrectionis,* the day before the resurrection; It is *Vigilia resurrectionis;* Our Easter Eve. *Adveniat regnum tuum,* possesse my soule of thy kingdom then: And, *Fiat voluntas tua* my body shall arise after, but how soon after, or how late after, thy will bee done then, by thy selfe, and thy will be knowne, till then, to thy selfe."[62] Idealizing as it is in its sketch of Donne's life and death, Walton's terse observation that near his end the Dean "closed many periods of his faint breath with these words, *Thy kingdome come, Thy will be done,*"[63] is certainly in harmony with not only Christian procedure but, and in particular, Donne's habitual use of petitions from the Lord's Prayer.

The famous *Death's Duell,* sub-titled "The Doctor's owne Funerall Sermon" by His Majesty's household, uses a strangely eloquent analogy.

Make this present day that [namely, Christ's last] day in thy devotion, and consider what hee did, and remember what you have done. . . . After the Sacrament hee spent the time till night in prayer, in preaching, in Psalmes. . . . At night hee went into the garden to pray, and he prayed prolixious he spent much time in prayer, how much? Because it is literally expressed, that he prayed there three severall times [margin: Luke 22, 24], and that returning to his Disciples after his first prayer, and finding them asleepe sayd, *could ye not watch with me one houre* [margin: Matt. 26, 40], it is collected that he spent three houres in prayer. I dare scarce aske thee whither thou wentest, or how thou

disposedst of thy self, when it grew darke and after last night: If
that time were spent in a holy recommendation of thy selfe to
God, and a submission of thy will to his, It was spent in a conformity to him. In that time and in those prayers was his agony
and bloody sweat. I will hope that thou didst pray; but not every
ordinary and customary prayer, but prayer actually accompanied
with shedding of teares, and dispositively in a readines to shed
blood for his glory in necessary cases, puts thee into a conformity
with him.[64]

Less austere is the same approach as found in one of the *Holy
Sonnets.*

> What if this present were the world's last night?
> Marke in my heart, O Soule, where thou dost dwell,
> The picture of Christ crucified, and tell
> Whether that countenance can thee affright,
> Teares in his eyes quench the amazing light,
> Blood fills his frownes, which from his pierc'd head fell.
> And can that tongue adjudge thee unto hell,
> Which pray'd forgivenesse for his foes' fierce spight?
> No, no; but as in my idolatrie
> I said to all my profane mistresses,
> Beauty, of pitty, foulnesse onely is
> A signe of rigour: so I say to thee,
> To wicked spirits are horrid shapes assign'd,
> This beauteous forme assures a pitious minde.[65]

These my introductory pages testify, almost entirely in John
Donne's own words as recorded in his poems, sermons, and
letters, what this man of the Renaissance wrote *about* prayer.
Clearly his is the Christian outlook which is definitely motivated
by the Bible. My main emphasis has shown that also before
his ordination into the ministry his prayer-life was active, and
that this spiritual quality in Donne flourished in his later years.
Thereby we can appreciate and understand better the energetic
vigor found in many of his lines, as well as the source of his
strength. How his friends must have welcomed not merely his

The Prayers of John Donne

literary products, but especially the soul-stimulus embodied in this thought expressed in a verse-letter "To Sir H[enry] W[otton] at his going Ambassador to Venice":

But though she [Fortune] part us, to heare my oft prayers
For your increase, God is as neere mee here;
And to send you what I shall begge, his staires
In length and ease are alike every where.[66]

The privilege of prayer meant, for Donne, including others as much as himself.

The naturally diverse and sometimes seemingly unrelated material in these preliminary pages has come from many contexts (and further investigation will show yet more passages that pertain), but there is an underlying coherence. We now know Donne's opinion of and convictions on private prayer and public worship, on human frailty and spiritual blessings despite misuses, on praise and prayer as the finest combination or blending, and on the Lord's Prayer together with Christ's example as the ideal submission of our desires to God's will. The main portion of this book—the actual prayers of Donne—should be much more significant now that we comprehend his devotional principles. "To which, he, whose name is Amen, say Amen, our blessed Saviour Christ Jesus, in the power of his Father, and in the operation of his Spirit."[67]

❧ The Prayers: Group 1 ❧

From *DIVINE POEMS,* composed after 1610, published in 1633 ff.

A. Deigne at my hands this crown of prayer and praise,
   Weav'd in my low devout melancholie,
   Thou which of good, hast, yea art treasury,
   All changing unchang'd Antient of dayes;
   But doe not, with a vile crowne of fraile bayes,
   Reward my muse's white sincerity,
   But what thy thorny crowne gain'd, that give mee,
   A crowne of Glory, which doth flower alwayes;
   The ends crowne our workes, but thou crown'st our ends,
   For, at our end begins our endlesse rest;
   The first last end, now zealously possest,
   With a strong sober thirst, my soule attends.
   'Tis time that heart and voice be lifted high,
   Salvation to all that will is nigh.

B. Salute the last and everlasting day,
   Joy at the uprising of this Sunne, and Sonne,
   Yee whose just teares, or tribulation
   Have purely washt, or burnt your drossie clay;
   Behold the Highest, parting hence away,
   Lightens the darke clouds, which hee treads upon,
   Nor doth hee by ascending, show alone,
   But first hee, and hee first enters the way.

O strong Ramme, which hast batter'd heaven for mee,
Mild Lambe, which with thy blood, hast mark'd the path;
Bright Torch, which shin'st, that I the way may see,
Oh, with thy owne blood quench thy owne just wrath,
And if thy holy Spirit, my Muse did raise,
Deigne at my hands this crowne of prayer and praise.

C. Thou hast made me, And shall thy worke decay?
Repaire me now, for now mine end doth haste,
I runne to death, and death meets me as fast,
And all my pleasures are like yesterday;
I dare not move my dimme eyes any way,
Despaire behind, and death before doth cast
Such terrour, and my feeble flesh doth waste
By sinne in it, which it t'wards hell doth weigh;
Onely thou art above, and when towards thee
By thy leave I can looke, I rise again;
But our old subtle foe so tempteth me,
That not one houre my selfe I can sustaine;
Thy Grace may wing me to prevent his art,
And thou like Adamant draw mine iron heart.

D. As due by many titles I resigne
My selfe to thee, O God, first I was made
By thee, and for thee, and when I was decay'd
Thy blood bought that, the which before was thine;
I am thy sonne, made with thy selfe to shine,
Thy servant, whose paines thou hast still repaid,
Thy sheepe, thine Image, and, till I betray'd
My selfe, a temple of thy Spirit divine;
Why doth the devill then usurpe on mee?
Why doth he steale, nay ravish that's thy right?
Except thou rise and for thine owne worke fight,
Oh I shall soone despaire, when I doe see
That thou lov'st mankind well, yet wilt'not chuse me,

And Satan hates mee, yet is loth to lose mee.

E. At the round earth's imagin'd corners, blow
   Your trumpets, Angells, and arise, arise
   From death, you numberlesse infinities
   Of soules, and to your scatt'red bodies goe,
   All whom the flood did, and fire shall o'erthrow,
   All whom warre, dearth, age, agues, tyrannies,
   Despaire, law, chance, hath slaine, and you whose eyes,
   Shall behold God, and never tast[e] death's woe.
   But let them sleepe, Lord, and mee mourne a space,
   For, if above all these, my sinnes abound,
   'Tis late to aske abundance of thy grace,
   When wee are there; here on this lowly ground,
   Teach mee how to repent; for that's as good
   As if thou'hadst seal'd my pardon, with thy blood.

F. Batter my heart, three person'd God; for, you
   As yet but knocke, breathe, shine, and seeke to mend;
   That I may rise, and stand, o'erthrow mee,' and bend
   Your force, to breake, blowe, burn and make me new.
   I, like an usurpt towne, to'another due,
   Labour to'admit you, but Oh, to no end,
   Reason your viceroy in mee, mee should defend,
   But is captiv'd, and proves weake or untrue.
   Yet dearely'I love you,'and would be loved faine,
   But am betroth'd unto your enemie:
   Divorce mee,'untie, or breake that knot againe,
   Take mee to you, imprison mee, for I
   Except you'enthrall mee, never shall be free,
   Nor ever chast[e], except you ravish mee,

G. Father, part of his double interest
   Unto thy kingdome, thy Sonne gives to mee,
   His joynture in the knottie Trinitie

Hee keepes, and gives to me his death's conquest.
This Lambe, whose death, with life the world hath blest,
Was from the world's beginning slaine, and he
Hath made two Wills, which with the Legacie
Of his and thy kingdome, doe thy Sonnes invest.
Yet such are thy laws, that men argue yet
Whether a man those statutes can fulfill;
None doth; but all-healing grace and spirit
Revive againe what law and letter kill.
Thy lawe's abridgement, and thy last command
Is all but love; Oh let this last Will stand!

H. Since she whom I lov'd hath pay'd her last debt
To Nature, and to hers, and my good is dead,
And her Soule early into heaven ravished,
Wholly on heavenly things my mind is sett.
Here the admyring her my mind did whett
To seeke thee God; so streames do shew their head;
But though I have found thee, and thou my thirst hast
    fed,
A holy thirsty dropsy melts mee yett.
But why should I begg more Love, when as thou
Dost wooe my soule for hers; off'ring all thine:
And dost not only feare least I allow
My Love to Saints and Angels things divine,
But in thy tender jealosy dost doubt
Least the World, Fleshe, yea Devill putt thee out.

I.   .   .   .

But that Christ on this Crosse, did rise and fall,
Sinne had eternally benighted all.
Yet dare I'almost be glad, I do not see
That spectacle of too much weight for mee.
Who sees God's face, that is selfe life, must dye;

46

The Prayers: Group One

What a death were it then to see God dye?
. . . .

Though these things, as I ride, be from mine eye,
They'are present yet unto my memory,
For that looks towards them; and thou look'st towards
    mee,
O Saviour, as thou hang'st upon the tree;
I turne my backe to thee, but to receive
Corrections, till thy mercies bid thee leave.
O thinke mee worth thine anger, punish mee,
Burne off my rusts, and my deformity,
Restore thine Image, so much, by thy grace,
That thou may'st know mee, and I'll turne my face.

J.   Father of Heaven, and him, by whom
    It, and us for it, and all else, for us
      Thou madest, and govern'st ever, come
And re-create mee, now growne ruinous:
      My heart is by dejection, clay,
      And by self-murder, red.
From this red earth, O Father, purge away
All vicious tinctures, that new fashioned
I may rise up from death, before I'm dead.

K.   O Sonne of God, who seeing two things,
    Sinne, and death crept in, which were never made,
      By bearing one, tryed'st with what stings
The other could thine heritage invade;
      O be thou nail'd unto my heart,
      And crucified againe,
Part not from it, though it from thee would part,
But let it be, by applying so thy paine,
Drown'd in thy blood, and in thy passion slaine.

L.   O Holy Ghost, whose temple I

Am, but of mudde walls, and condensed dust,
    And being sacrilegiously
Halfe wasted with youth's fires, of pride and lust,
    Must with new stormes be weatherbeat;
    Double in my heart thy flame,
Which let devout sad teares intend; and let
(Though this glasse lanthorne, flesh, do suffer maime)
Fire, Sacrifice, Priest, Altar be the same.

M.   O Blessed glorious Trinity,
Bones to Philosophy, but milke to faith,
    Which, as wise serpents, diversly
Most slipperinesse, yet most entanglings hath,
    As you distinguish'd undistinct
    By power, love, knowledge bee,
Give mee a such selfe different instinct
Of these; let all mee elemented bee,
Of power, to love, to know, you unnumb'red three.

N.   Heare us, O heare us Lord; to thee
A sinner is more musique, when he prayes,
    Than spheares, or Angels' praises bee,
In Panegyrique Allelujaes;
    Heare us, for till thou heare us, Lord
    We know not what to say;
Thine eare to'our sighes, teares, thoughts gives voice
    and word.
O Thou who Satan heard'st in Job's sicke day.
Heare thy selfe now, for thou in us dost pray.

O.   That wee may change to evennesse
This intermitting aguish Pietie;
    That snatching cramps of wickednesse
And Apoplexies of fast sin, may die;

That musique of thy promises,
Not threats in Thunder may
Awaken us to our just offices;
What in thy booke, thou dost, or creatures say,
That we may heare, Lord heare us, when wee pray.

P.   Sonne of God heare us, and since thou
By taking our blood, owest it us againe,
    Gaine to thy selfe, or us allow;
And let not both us and thy selfe be slaine;
      O Lambe of God, which took'st our sinne
      Which could not stick to thee,
O let it not returne to us againe,
But Patient and Physition being free,
As sinne is nothing, let it no where be.

Q. Eternall God, (for whom who ever dare
Seeke new expressions, doe the Circle square,
And thrust into strait corners of poore wit
Thee, who art cornerlesse and infinite)
I would but blesse thy Name, not name thee now;
(And thy gifts are as infinite as thou:)
Fixe we our prayses therefore on this one,
That, as thy blessed Spirit fell upon
These Psalmes' first Author in a cloven tongue;
(For 'twas a double power by which he sung
The highest matter in the noblest forme;)
So thou hast cleft that spirit, to performe
That worke againe, and shed it, here, upon
Two, by their bloods, and by thy Spirit one;
A Brother and a Sister, made by thee
The Organ, where thou art the Harmony.

.   .   .   .

So though some have, some may some Psalmes translate,

The Prayers of John Donne

We thy Sydnean Psalmes shall celebrate,
And, till we come th'Extemporall song to sing,
(Learn'd the first hower, that we see the King,
Who hath translated those translators) may
These their sweet learned labours, all the way
Be as our tuning; that, when hence we part,
We may fall in with them, and sing our part.

R. In what torne ship soever I embarke,
That ship shall be my embleme of thy Arke;
What sea soever swallow mee, that flood
Shall be to mee an embleme of thy blood;
Though thou with clouds of anger do disguise
Thy face; yet through that maske I know those eyes,
Which, though they turne away sometimes,
They never will despise.

I sacrifice this Iland unto thee,
And all whom I lov'd there, and who lov'd mee;
When I have put our seas 'twixt them and mee,
Put thou thy sea betwixt my sinnes and thee.
As the tree's sap doth seeke the root below
In winter, in my winter now I goe,
Where none but thee, th'Eternall root
Of true Love I may know.

Nor thou nor thy religion dost controule,
The amorousnesse of an harmonious Soule,
But thou would'st have that love thy selfe: As thou
Art jealous, Lord, so I am jealous now,
Thou lov'st not, till from loving more, thou free
My soule: Who ever gives, takes libertie:
O, if thou car'st not whom I love
Alas, thou lov'st not mee.

Seale then this bill of my Divorce to All,

On whom those fainter beames of love did fall;
Marry those loves, which in youth scattered bee
On Fame, Wit, Hopes (false mistresses) to thee.
Churches are best for Prayer, that have least light:
To see God only, I goe out of sight:
    And to 'scape stormy dayes, I chuse
    An Everlasting night.

S. . . . .

I am the man which have affliction seene,
Under the rod of God's wrath having beene,

. . . .

My soule is humbled in rememb'ring this;
My heart considers, therefore, hope there is.
'Tis God's great mercy we'are not utterly
Consum'd, for his compassions do not die;

For every morning they renewed bee,
For great, O Lord, is thy fidelity.
The Lord is, saith my Soule, my portion,
And therefore in him will I hope alone.

The Lord is good to them, who on him relie,
And to the Soule that seeks him earnestly.
It is both good to trust, and to attend
(The Lord's salvation) unto the end:

. . . .

Remember, O Lord, what is fallen on us;
See, and marke how we are reproached thus,

. . . .

Now is the crowne falne from our head; and woe

Be unto us, because we'have sinned so.
For this our hearts do languish, and for this
Over our eyes a cloudy dimnesse is.

Because mount Sion desolate doth lye,
And foxes there do goe at libertie:
But thou O Lord art ever, and thy throne
From generation, to generation.

Why should'st thou forget us eternally?
Or leave us thus long in this misery?
Restore us Lord to thee, that so we may
Returne, and as of old, renew our day.

For oughtest thou, O Lord, despise us thus,
And to be utterly enrag'd at us?

T. Since I am comming to that Holy roome,
　　　Where, with thy Quire of Saints for evermore,
I shall be made thy Musique; As I come
　　　I tune the Instrument here at the dore,
　　　And what I must doe then, thinke here before.

Whilst my Physitians by their love are growne
　　　Cosmographers, and I their Mapp, who lie
Flat on this bed, that by them may be showne
　　　That this is my South-west discoverie
　　　Per fretum febris, by these streights to die,

I joy, that in these straits, I see my West;
　　　For, though theire currants yeeld returne to none,
What shall my West hurt me? As West and East
　　　In all flatt Maps (and I am one) are one,

The Prayers: Group One

So death doth touch the Resurrection.
Is the Pacifique Sea my home? Or are
    The Easterne riches? Is Ierusalem?
Anyan, and Magellan, and Gibraltare,
    All streights, and none but streights, are wayes
      to them,
    Whether where Iaphet dwelt, or Cham, or Sem.

We thinke that Paradise and Calvarie,
    Christ's Crosse, and Adam's tree, stood in one
      place;
Looke Lord, and finde both Adams met in me;
    As the first Adam's sweat surrounds my face,
    May the last Adam's blood my soule embrace.

So, in his purple wrapp'd receive mee Lord,
    By these his thornes give me his other Crowne;
And as to others' soules I preach'd thy word,
    Be this my Text, my Sermon to mine owne,
    Therfore that he may raise the Lord throws down.

U. Wilt thou forgive that sinne where I begunne,
    Which was my sin, though it were done before?
Wilt thou forgive that sinne, through which I runne,
    And do run still: though still I do deplore?
      When thou hast done, thou hast not done,
        For I have more

Wilt thou forgive that sinne which I have wonne
    Others to sinne? and, made my sinne their doore?
Wilt thou forgive that sinne which I did shunne
    A yeare, or two: but wallowed in, a score?
      When thou hast done, thou hast not done,
        For, I have more.

The Prayers of John Donne

I have a sinne of feare, that when I have spunne
My last thred, I shall perish on the shore;
But sweare by thy selfe, that at my death thy sonne
Shall shine as he shines now, and heretofore;
And, having done that, Thou haste done,
I feare no more.

❧ The Prayers: Group 2 ❧

From *ESSAYES IN DIVINITY* . . . , composed about
1615, published in 1651

A.   In the Beginning whereof [i.e. Genesis], O onely Eternall God, of whose being, beginning, or lasting, this beginning
is no period, nor measure; which art no Circle, for thou hast no
ends to close up; which art not within this All, for it cannot comprehend thee; nor without it, for thou fillest it; nor art it thy
self, for thou madest it; which having decreed from all eternity,
to do thy great work of Mercy, our Redemption in the fulnesse
of time, didst now create time it selfe to conduce to it; and
madest thy glory and thy mercy equal thus, that though thy
glorious work of Creation were first, thy mercifull work of Redemption was greatest. Let me in thy beloved Servant Augustine's own words [margin: Conf[essions]. li. c.3.], when with
an humble boldnesse he begg'd the understanding of this passage, say, Moses writ this, but is gon from me to thee; if he were
here, I would hold him, and beseech him for thy sake, to tell
me what he meant. If he spake Hebrew, he would frustrate my
hope; but if Latine, I should comprehend him. But from whence
should I know that he said true? Or when I knew it, came
that knowledge from him? No, for within me, within me there
is a truth, not Hebrew, nor Greek, nor Latin, nor barbarous;
which without organs, without noyse of Syllables, tels me true,
and would enable me to say confidently to Moses, Thou say'st
true. . . . it is an Article of our Belief, that the world began.
And therefore for this point, we are not under the insinuations

and mollifyings of perswasion, and conveniency; nor under the reach and violence of Argument, or Demonstration, or Necessity; but under the Spirituall, and peaceable Tyranny, and easie yoke of sudden and present Faith. . . .

B.   O Eternall and Almighty power, which being infinite, hast enabled a limited creature, Faith, to comprehend thee; And being, even to Angels but a passive Mirror and looking-glasse, art to us an Active guest and domestick, (for thou hast said [margin: Rev. 3, 20], *I stand at the door and knock, if any man hear me, and open the doore, I will come in unto him, and sup with him, and he with me*), and so thou dwell'st in our hearts; And not there only, but even in our mouths; for though thou bee'st greater and more remov'd, yet humbler and more communicable than the Kings of Egypt, or Roman Emperours, which disdain'd their particular distinguishing Names, for Pharaoh and Caesar, names of confusion; hast contracted thine immensity, and shut thy selfe within Syllables, and accepted a Name from us; O keep and defend my tongue from misusing that Name in lightnesse, passion, or falshood; and my heart, from mistaking thy Nature, by an inordinate preferring thy Justice before thy Mercy, or advancing this before that. And as, though thy self hadst no beginning thou gavest a beginning to all things in which thou wouldst be served and glorified; so, though this soul of mine, by which I partake thee, begin not now, yet let this minute, O God, this happy minute of thy visitation, be the beginning of her conversion, and shaking away confusion, darknesse, and barrennesse; and let her now produce Creatures, thoughts, words, and deeds agreeable to thee. And let her not produce them, O God, out of any contemplation, or (I cannot say, Idaea), but Chimera of my worthinesse, either because I am a man and no worme, and within the pale of thy Church, and not in the wild forrest, and enlight'ned with some glimerings of Naturall knowledge; but meerely out of Nothing: Nothing preexistent in her selfe, but by power of thy Divine will and word. By which, as thou didst so make Heaven, as thou didst not neglect Earth, and madest them answerable and agreeable to one another, so let my Soul's Creatures have that temper and Harmony, that they be not by a misdevout consideration of the next life, stupidly and trecherously negligent of the offices and duties which thou enjoynest amongst us in this life; nor so anxious in these, that the other (which is our better business, though this also must be attended) be the less endeavoured. Thou hast, O God, denied even to Angells, the ability of arriving from one Extreme to another, without passing the mean way between. Nor can we pass from the prison of our Mother's womb, to thy palace, but we must walk (in that pace whereto thou hast enabled us) through the street of this life, and not sleep at the first corner, nor in the midst. Yet since my soul is sent immediately from thee, (let me for her return) rely, not principally, but wholly upon thee and thy word: and for this body, made of preordained matter, and instruments, let me so use the materiall means of her sustaining, that I neither neglect the seeking, nor grudge the missing of the Conveniencies of this life: And that for fame, which is a mean Nature between them, I so esteem opinion, that I despise not others' thoughts of me, since most men are such, as most men think they be: nor so reverence it, that I make it always the rule of my Actions. And because in this world my Body was first made, and then my Soul, but in the next my soul shall be first, and then my body, In my Exterior and morall conversation let my first and presentest care be to give them satisfaction with whom I am mingled, because they may be scandaliz'd, but thou, which seest hearts, canst not: But for my faith, let my first relation be to thee, because of that thou art justly jealous, which they cannot be. Grant these requests, O God, if I have asked fit things fitly, and as many more, under the same limitations, as are within that prayer which (as thy Manna [margin: Sap. 16, 20], which was meat for all tast[e]s, and served to the appetite of him which took it, and was that which every man would) includes all which all can aske, *Our Father which art,* etc.

C.   O Eternall God, as thou didst admit thy faithfull servant Abraham, to make the granting of one petition an incouragement and rise to another, and gavest him leave to gather upon thee from fifty to ten; so I beseech thee, that since by thy grace, I have thus long meditated upon thee, and spoken of thee, I may now speak to thee. As thou hast enlight'ned and enlarged me to contemplate thy greatness, so, O God, descend thou and stoop down to see my infirmities and the Egypt in which I live; and (If thy good pleasure be such) hasten mine Exodus and deliverance, for I desire to be, disolved, and be with thee. O Lord, I most humbly acknowledg and confess thine infinite Mercy, that when thou hadst almost broke the staff of bread, and called a famine of thy word almost upon all the world, then thou broughtest me into this Egypt, where thou hadst appointed thy stewards to husband thy blessings, and to feed thy flock. Here also, O God, thou hast multiplied thy children in me, by begetting and cherishing in me reverent devotions, and pious affections towards thee, but that mine own corruption, mine own Pharaoh hath ever smothered and strangled them. And thou hast put me in my way towards thy land of promise, thy Heavenly Canaan, by removing me from the Egypt of frequented and populous, glorious places, to a more solitary and desart retiredness, where I may more safely feed upon both thy Mannaes, thy self in thy Sacrament, and that other, which is true Angells' food, contemplation of thee. O Lord, I most humbly acknowledg and confess, that I feel in me so many strong effects of thy Power, as only for the Ordinariness and frequency thereof, they are not Miracles. For hourly thou rectifiest my lameness, hourly thou

restorest my sight, and hourly not only deliverest me from the
Egypt, but raisest me from the death of sin. My sin, O God,
hath not onely caused thy descent hither, and passion here; but
by it I am become that hell into which thou descendedst after thy
Passion; yea, after thy glorification: for hourly thou in thy
Spirit descendest into my heart, to overthrow there Legions of
spirits of Disobedience, and Incredulity, and Murmuring. O
Lord, I most humbly acknowledg and confesse, that by thy Mercy
I have a sense of thy Justice; for not onely those afflictions with
which it pleaseth thee to exercise mee, awaken me to consider
how terrible thy severe justice is; but even the rest and security
which thou affordest mee, puts me often into fear, that thou re-
servest and sparest me for a greater measure of punishment. O
Lord, I most humbly acknowledg and confesse, that I have under-
stood sin, by understanding thy laws and judgments; but have
done against thy known and revealed will. Thou hast set up
many candlesticks, and kindled many lamps in mee; but I have
either blown them out, or carried them to guide me in by and
forbidden ways. Thou hast given mee a desire of knowledg,
and some meanes to it, and some possession of it; and I have
arm'd my self with thy weapons against thee: Yet, O God, have
mercy upon me, for thine own sake have mercy upon me. Let
not sin and me be able to exceed thee, nor to defraud thee, nor
to frustrate thy purposes: But let me, in despite of Me, be of so
much use to thy glory, that by thy mercy to my sin, other sinners
may see how much sin thou canst pardon. Thus show mercy to
many in one: And shew thy power and al-mightinesse upon thy
self, by casting manacles upon thine own hands, and calling back
those Thunder-bolts which thou hadst thrown against me.
Show thy Justice upon the common Seducer and Devourer of us
all: and show to us so much of thy Judgments, as may instruct,
not condemn us. Hear us, O God, hear us, for this contrition
which thou hast put into us, who come to thee with that watch-
word, by which thy Son hath assured us of access. *Our Father
which art in Heaven,* etc.

D.   O Eternall God, who art not only first and last, but in whom, first and last is all one, who art not only all Mercy, and all Justice, but in whom Mercy and Justice is all one; who in the height of thy Justice, wouldest not spare thine own, and only most innocent Son; and yet in the depth of thy mercy, would'st not have the wretched'st liver come to destruction; Behold us, O God, here gathered together in thy fear, according to thine ordinance, and in confidence of thy promise, that when two or three are gathered together in thy name, thou wilt be in the midst of them, and grant them their petitions. We confess O God, that we are not worthy so much as to confess; less to be heard, least of all to be pardoned our manifold sins and transgressions against thee. We have betrayed thy Temples to prophaness, our bodies to sensuality, thy fortresses to thine enemy, our soules to Satan. We have armed him with thy munition to fight against thee, by surrend'ring our eyes, and eares, all our senses, all our faculties to be exercised and wrought upon, and tyrannized by him. Vanities and disguises have covered us, and thereby we are naked; licenciousness hath inflam'd us, and thereby we are frozen; voluptuousness hath fed us, and thereby we are sterved, the fancies and traditions of men have taught and instructed us, and thereby we are ignorant. These distempers, thou only, O God, who art true, and perfect harmonie, canst tune, and rectify, and set in order again. Doe so then, O most Merciful Father, for thy most innocent Son's sake: and since he hath spread his armes upon the cross, to receive the whole world, O Lord, shut out none of us (who are now fallen before the throne of thy Majesty and thy Mercy) from the benefit of his merits; but with as many of us, as begin their conversion and newness of life, this minute, this minute, O God, begin thou thy account with them, and put all that is past out of thy remembrance. Accept our humble thanks for all thy Mercies; and, continue and enlarge them upon the whole Church, etc.

The Prayers: Group Two

E.   O most glorious and most gracious God, into whose presence our own consciences make us afraid to come, and from whose presence we cannot hide our selves, hide us in the wounds of thy Son, our Saviour Christ Jesus; And though our sins be as red as scarlet, give them there another redness, which may be acceptable in thy sight. We renounce, O Lord, all our confidence in this world; for this world passeth away, and the lusts thereof: Wee renounce all our confidence in our own merits for we have done nothing in respect of that which we might have done; neither could we ever have done any such thing, but that still we must have remained unprofitable servants to thee; we renounce all confidence, even in our own confessions, and accusations of our self; for our sins are above number, if we would reckon them; above weight and measure, if we would weigh and measure them; and past finding out, if we would seek them in those dark corners, in which we have multiplied them against thee: yea we renounce all confidence even in our repentances; for we have found by many lamentable experiences, that we never perform our promises to thee, never perfect our purposes in our selves, but relapse again and again into those sins which again and again we have repented. We have no confidence in this world, but in him who hath taken possession of the next world for us, by sitting down at thy right hand. We have no confidence in our merits, but in him, whose merits thou hast been pleased to accept for us, and to apply to us, we have: no confidence in our own confessions and repentances, but in that blessed Spirit, who is the Author of them, and loves to perfect his own works and build upon his own foundations, we have: Accept them therefore, O Lord, for their sakes whose they are; our poor endeavours, for thy glorious Son's sake, who gives them their root, and so they are his; our poor beginnings of sanctification, for thy blessed Spirit's sake, who gives them their growth, and so they are his: and for thy Son's sake, in whom only our prayers

are acceptable to thee: and for thy Spirit's sake which is now
in us, and must be so whensoever we do pray acceptably to thee;
accept our humble prayers for, etc.

F.   O Eternal and most merciful God, against whom, as we
know and acknowledg that we have multiplied contemptuous
and rebellious sins, so we know and acknowledg too, that it
were a more sinfull contempt and rebellion, than all those, to
doubt of thy mercy for them; have mercy upon us: In the merits
and mediation of thy Son, our Saviour Christ Jesus, be mercifull
unto us. Suffer not, O Lord, so great a waste, as the effusion of
his blood, without any return to thee; suffer not the expence of
so rich a treasure, as the spending of his life, without any pur-
chace to thee; but as thou didst empty and evaouate [evacuate]
his glory here upon earth, glorify us with that glory which his
humiliation purchased for us in the kingdom of Heaven. And
as thou didst empty that Kingdome of thine, in a great part, by
the banishment of those Angels, whose pride threw them into
everlasting ruine, be pleased to repair that Kingdom, which their
fall did so far depopulate, by assuming us into their places, and
making us rich with their confiscations. And to that purpose, O
Lord, make us capable of that succession to thine Angels there;
begin in us here in this life an angelicall purity, an angelicall
chastity, an angelicall integrity to thy service, an Angelicall ack-
nowledgment that we alwaies stand in thy presence, and should
direct all our actions to thy glory. Rebuke us not, O Lord, in
thine anger, that we have not done so till now; but enable us now
to begin that great work; and imprint in us an assurance that
thou receivest us now graciously, as reconciled, though enemies;
and fatherly, as children, though prodigals; and powerfully,
as the God of our Salavation, though our own consciences testifie
against us. Continue and enlarge thy blessings upon the whole
Church, etc.

❧ The Prayers: Group 3 ❧

From *DEVOTIONS UPON EMERGENT OCCASIONS . . . ,* composed in 1623, published in 1624 ff.

A.   O Eternall, and most gracious God, who considered in thy selfe, art a Circle, first and last, and altogether; but considered in thy working upon us, art a direct line, and leadest us from our beginning, through all our wayes, to our end, enable me by thy grace, to looke forward to mine end, and to looke backward to[o], to the cõ[n]siderations of thy mercies afforded mee from the beginning; that so by that practise of considering thy mercy, in my beginning in this world, when thou plã[n]tedst me in the Christian Church, and thy mercy in the beginning in the other world, whẽ[n] thou writest me in the Booke of life, in my Election, I may come to a holy consideration of thy mercy, in the beginning of all my actions here: That in all the beginnings, in all the accesses, and approches of spirituall sicknesses of Sinn, I may heare and hearken to that voice [margin: 2 Reg. 4, 40], *O thou Man of God, there is death in the pot,* and so re-fraine from that, which I was so hungerly, so greedily flying to. *A faithfull Ambassador is health,* says thy wise servant *Solomon* [margin: Prov. 13, 17]. Thy voice received, in the beginning of a sicknesse, of a sinne, is true health. If I can see that light betimes, and heare that voyce early, *Then shall my light breake forth as the morning, and my health shall spring foorth speedily* [margin: Esa. 58, 8].

Deliver mee therefore, O my God, from these vaine imagina-tions; that it is an overcurious thing, a dangerous thing, to come

to that tendernesse, that rawnesse, that scrupulousnesse, to feare
every concupiscence, every offer of Sin, that this suspicious, and
iealous diligence will turne to an inordinate deiection of spirit,
and a diffidence in thy care and providence; but keep me still
establish'd, both in a constant assurance, that thou wilt speake
to me at the beginning of every such sicknes, at the approach of
every such Sinne; and that, if I take knowledg of that voice
then, and flye to thee, thou wilt preserve mee from falling, or
raise me againe, when by naturall infirmitie I am fallen: doe this,
O Lord, for his sake, who knowes our naturall infirmities, for
he had them; and knowes the weight of our sinns, for he paid a
deare price for them, thy Sonne, our Saviour, Chr: Iesus, Amen.

B.   O Eternall, and most gracious God, who calledst down
fire from Heaven upon the sinfull Cities, but once, and open-
edst the Earth to swallow the Murmurers, but once, and
threwst down the Tower of Siloe upon sinners, but once, but
for thy workes of mercie repeatest them often, and still workest
by thine owne paternes, as thou broghtest Man into this world,
by giving him a Helper fit for him here, so whether it bee thy
will to continue mee long thus, or to dismisse me by death, be
pleased to afford me the helpes fit for both conditions, either for
my weak stay here, or my finall transmigration from hence. And
if thou mayest receive glory by that way (and, by all wayes thou
maist receive glory) glorifie thy selfe in preserving this body
from such infections, as might withhold those, who would come,
or indanger thē[m] who doe come; and preserve this soule in
the faculties thereof, frõ[m] all such distempers, as might shake
the assurance which my selfe and others have had, that because
thou hast loved me, thou wouldst love me to my end, and at my
end. Open none of my dores, not of my h[e]art, not of mine
eares, not of my house, to any supplanter that would enter to
undermine me in my Religion to thee, in the time of my weaknesse, or to defame me, and magnifie himselfe, with false rumors

of such a victory, and surprisall of me, after I am dead; Be my salvation, and plead my salvation; work it, and declare it; and as thy triumphant shall be, so let the Militant Church bee assured, that thou wast my God, and I thy servant, to, and in my consummation. Blesse thou the learning, and the labours of this Man [the physician], whō[m] thou sendest to assist me; and since thou takest mee by the hand, and puttest me into his hands (for I come to him in thy name, who, in thy name comes to me) since I clog not my hopes in him, no nor my prayers to thee, with any limited conditions, but inwrap all in those two petitions, *Thy kingdome come, thy will be done,* prosper him, and relieve me, in thy way, in thy time, and in thy measure. Amen.

C.　　O Most mightie God and mercifull God, the God of all true sorrow, and true ioy to[o], of all feare, and of all hope to[o], as thou hast given me a Repentance, not to be repented of, so give me, O Lord, a feare, of which I may not be afraid. Give me tender, and supple, and conformable affections, that as I ioy with them that ioy, and mourne with them, that mourne, so I may feare with them that feare. And since thou hast vouchsafed to discover to me, in his [the physician's] feare whom thou hast admitted to be my assistance, in this sicknesse, that there is danger therein, let me not, O Lord, go about to overcome the sense of that fear, so far, as to pretermit the fitting, and preparing of my selfe, for the worst that may bee fear'd, the passage out of this life. Many of thy blessed Martyrs, have passed out of this life, without any showe of feare; But thy most blessed Sonne himselfe did not so. Thy Martyrs were known to be but men, and therfore it pleased thee, to fill thē[m] with thy Spirit, and thy power, in that they did more than Men; Thy Son was declar'd by thee, and by himselfe to be God; and it was requisite, that he should declare himselfe to be Man also, in the weaknesses of man. Let mee not therefore, O my God, bee ashamed of these feares, but let me feele them to determine, where his feare

65

did, in a present submitting of all to thy will. And when thou shalt have inflam'd, and thaw'd my former coldnesses, and indevotions, with these heats, and quenched my former heates, with these sweats, and inundations, and rectified my former presumptions, and neglicences with these fears, bee pleased, O Lord, as one, made so by thee, to thinke me fit for thee; And whether it be thy pleasure, to dispose of this body, this garment so, as to put it to a farther wearing in this world, or to lay it up in the common wardrope, the grave, for the next, glorifie thy selfe in thy choyce now, and glorifie it then, with that glory, which thy Son, our Saviour Christ Iesus hath purchased for them, whome thou makest partakers of his Resurrection. Amen.

D. O Eternall and most gracious God, who though thou have reserved thy tresure of perfit ioy, and perfit glory, to be given by thine own hands then, whē[n] by seeing thee, as thou art in thy selfe, and knowing thee, as we are known, wee shall possesse in an instant, and possesse for ever, all that can any way cō[n]duce to our happinesses, yet here also in this world, givest us such earnests of that full payment, as by the value of the earnest, we may give some estimat of the tresure, humbly, and thā[n]kfully I acknowledge, that thy blessed spirit instructs mee, to make a differē[n]ce of thy blessings in this world, by that difference of the Instruments, by which it hath pleased thee to derive them unto me. As we see thee heere in a glasse, so we receive frō[m] thee here by reflexion, and by instruments. Even casual things come from thee; and that which we call Fortune here, hath another name above. Nature reaches out her hand, and gives us corne and wine, and oyle, and milk, but thou fillest her hand before, and thou openest her hand, that she may rain down her showres upon us. Industry reaches out her hand to us, and gives us fruits of our labor, for our selves, and our posteritie; but thy hand guides that hand, when it sowes, and when it waters, and the increase is from thee. Friends reach out their hands, and prefer us, but thy hand supports that hã[n]d, that supports us. Of all these thy instruments have I received thy blessing, O God, but bless thy name most for the greatest; that as a member of the publike, and as a partaker of private favours too, by thy right hand, thy powerfull hand set over us, I have had my portion, not only in the hearing, but in the preaching of thy Gospel. [I am] Humbly beseeching thee, that as thou continuest thy wonted goodnes upon the whol world, by the wonted meanes, and instruments, the same Sun, and Moon, the same Nature, and Industry, so to continue the same blessings upon this State, and this Church by the same hand, so long, as that thy Son when he comes in the clouds, may find him [the King of England], or his Son, or his sonnes' sonnes ready to give an account, and able to stand in that iudg-mē[n]t, for their faithfull Stewardship, and dispensation of thy talē[n]ts so abũ[n]dantly cõ[m]mitted to them; and be to him, O God, in all distē[m] pers of his body, in all anxieties of spirit, in all holy sadnesses of soule, such a Phisician in thy pro-portion, who art the greatest in heaven, as hee hath bin in soule, and body to me, in his proportiõ[n], who is the great'st upon earth.

E.   O Eternall and most gracious God, who art of so pure eyes, as that thou canst not look upon sinn, and we of so unpure constitutions, as that wee can present no obiect but sin, and therefore might iustly feare, that thou wouldst turn thine eyes for ever from us, as, though we cannot indure afflictions in our selves, yet in thee we can; so tho[u]gh thou canst not in-dure sinne in us, yet in thy Sonn thou canst, and he hath taken upon him selfe, and presented to thee, al[l] those sins, which might displease thee in us. There is an Eye in Nature, that kills, as soon as it sees, [namely] the eye of a Serpent; no eye in Nature, that nourishes us by looking upon us; But thine Eye, O Lord, does so. Looke therefore upon me, O Lord, in this distresse, and that will recall mee from the borders of this bodily death; Look upon me, and that wil[l] raise me again from that spirituall death, in which my parents buried me, when they begot mee in sinne, and in which I have pierced even to the iawes of hell, by multiplying such heaps of actuall sins, upon that foundation, that root of originall sinn. Yet take me again, into your Consultation, O blessed and glorious Trinitie; and tho[u]gh the Father know, that I have defaced his Image received in my Creation; though the Sonn know, I have neglected mine interest in the Redemption, yet, O blessed spirit, as thou art to my Consciē[n]ce, so be to them a witnes, that at this minute, I accept that which I have so often, so often, so rebelliously refused, thy blessed inspirations; be thou my witnes to them, that at more poores [pores] than this slacke body sweates teares, this sad soule weeps blood; and more for the displeasure of my God, than for the stripes of his displeasure. Take me then, O blessed, and glorious Trinitie, into a Recō[n]-sultation, and prescribe me any phisick; If it bee a long, and painful holding of this soule in sicknes, it is phisick, if I may discern thy hand to give it, and it is phisick, if it be a speedy departing of this Soule, if I may discerne thy hand to receive it.

F.   O Eternall and most gracious God, who art able to make, and dost make the sicke bed of thy servants, Chappels of ease to them, and the dreames of thy servants, Prayers, and Meditations upon thee, let not this continuall watchfulnes of mine, this inabilitie to sleepe, which thou hast laid upon mee, be any disquiet or discomfort to me, but rather an argument, that thou wouldest not have me sleepe in thy presence. What it may indicate or signifie, concerning the state of my body, let them consider to whom that consideration belongs; doe thou, who onely art the Physitian of my soule, tell her, that thou wilt afford her such defensatives as that shee shall wake ever towards thee, and yet ever sleepe in thee; and that through all this sicknesse, thou wilt either preserve mine understanding from all decaies and distractions, which these watchings might occasion, or that thou wilt reckon, and account with me, from before those violencies, and not call any peece of my sicknesse, a sinne. It is a heavy, and indelible sinne, that I brought into the world with me; It is a heavy and innumerable multitude of sins, which I have heaped up since; I have sinned behind thy backe (if that can be done) by wilfull absteining from thy Congregations, and omitting thy service, and I have sinned before thy face, in my hypocrisies in Prayer, in my ostentation, and the mingling a respect of my selfe, in preaching thy Word; I have sinned in my fasting by repining, when a penurious fortune hath kept mee low; and I have sinned even in that fulnesse, when I have been at thy table, by a negligent examination, by a wilfull prevarication, in receiving that heavenly food and Physicke. But, as I know, O my gracious God, that for all those sinnes committed since, yet thou wilt consider me, as I was in thy purpose, when thou wrotest my name in the Booke of Life, in mine Election: so into what deviations soever I stray, and wander, by occasion of this sicknes, O God, returne thou to that Minute, wherein thou wast pleased with me, and consider me in that condition.

G.   O Eternall and most gracious God, who hast beene pleased to speake to us, not onely in the voice of Nature, who speakes in our hearts, and of thy word, which speakes to our eares, but in the speech of speechlesse Creatures, in Balaam's Asse, in the speech of unbeleeving men, in the confession of Pilate, in the speech of the Devill himselfe, in the recognition and attestation of thy Sonne, I humbly accept thy voice in the sound of this sad and funerall bell. And first, I blesse thy glorious name, that in this sound and voice I can heare thy instructions, in another man's to consider mine own condition; and to know, that this bell which tolls for another, before it come to ring out, may take in me too. As death is the wages of sinne, it is due to mee;

as death is the end of sicknesse, it belongs to mee; And though so disobedient a servant as I, may be afraid to die, yet to so mercifull a Master as thou, I cannot be afraid to come; And therefore, *into thy hands*, O my God, *I commend my spirit;* A surrender, which I know thou wilt accept, whether I live or die; for thy servant David [margin: Psalm 31, 5] made it, when he put himselfe into thy protection for his life; and thy blessed Sonne made it, when hee delivered up his soule at his death; declare thou thy will upon mee, O Lord, for life or death, in thy time; receive my surrender of my selfe, now, *Into thy hands,* O Lord, *I commend my spirit.* And being thus, O my God, pre-pared by thy correction, mellowed by thy chastisement, and con-formed to thy will, by thy Spirit, having received thy pardon for my soule, and asking no reprieve for my Body, I am bold, O Lord, to bend my prayers to thee, for his assistance, the voice of whose bell hath called mee to this devotion. Lay hold upon his soule, O God, till that soule have th[o]roughly considered his account, and how few minutes soever it have to remaine in that body, let the power of thy Spirit recompence the shortnesse of time, and perfect his account, before he passe away: present his sinnes so to him, as that he may know what thou forgivest, and not doubt of thy forgivenesse; let him stop upon the infinitenesse of those sinnes, but dwell upon the infinitenesse of thy Mercy: let him discerne his owne demerits, but wrap himselfe up in the merits of thy Sonne, Christ Jesus: Breath[e] inward comforts to his heart, and affoord him the power of giving such outward testi-monies thereof, as all that are about him may derive comforts from thence, and have this edification, even in this dissolution, that though the body be going the way of all flesh, yet that soule is going the way of all Saints. When thy Sonne cried out upon the Crosse, *My God, my God, Why hast thou forsaken me?* he spake not so much in his owne Person, as in the person of the Church, and of his afflicted members, who in deep distresses might feare thy forsaking. This patient, O most blessed God, is one of them; in his behalfe, and in his name, heare thy Sonne crying to thee, *My God, my God, why hast thou forsaken me?* and forsake him not; but with thy left hand lay his body in the grave, (if that bee thy determination upon him) and with thy right hand receive his soule into thy Kingdome, and unite him and us in one Cõ[m]munion of Saints. Amen.

H.   O Eternall and most gracious God, who hast made little things to signifie great, and convaid the infinite merits of thy Sonne in the water of Baptisme, and in the Bread and Wine of thy other Sacrament, unto us, receive the sacrifice of my humble thanks, that thou hast not onely afforded mee, the abilitie to rise out of this bed of wearinesse and discomfort, but hast also made this bodily rising, by thy grace, an earnest of a second resurrection from sinne, and of a third, to everlasting glory. Thy Sonne himselfe, alwaies infinite in himselfe, and incapable of addition, was yet pleased to grow in the Virgin's wombe, and to grow in stature, in the sight of men. Thy good purposes upon mee, I know, have their determination and perfection, in thy holy will upon mee; there thy grace is, and there I am altogether; but manifest thẽ[m] so unto me, in thy seasons, and in thy measures and degrees, that I may not onely have that comfort of knowing thee to be infinitely good, but that also of finding thee to be every day better and better to mee: and that as thou gavest Saint Paul, the Messenger of Satan, to humble him, so for my humiliation, thou maiest give me thy selfe, in this knowledge, that what grace soever thou afford mee to day, yet I should perish to morrow, if I had not to morrowe's grace too. Therefore I begge of thee, my daily bread; and as thou gavest mee the bread of sorrow for many daies, and since the bread of hope for some, and this day the bread of possessing, in rising by that strength, which thou the God of all strength, hast infused into me, so, O Lord, continue to mee the bread of life; the spiritual bread of life, in a faithfull assurance in thee; the sacramentall bread of life, in a worthy receiving of thee; and the more reall bread of life, in an everlasting union to thee. I know, O Lord, that when thou hadst created Angels, and they saw thee produce fowle, and fish, and beasts, and wormes, they did not importune thee, and say, shall wee have no better Creatures than these, no better companions than these; but staid thy leisure, and then had man delivered over to them, not much inferiour in nature to themselves. No more doe I, O God, now that by thy first mercie, I am able to rise, importune thee for present confirmation of health; nor now, that by thy mercie, I am brought to see, that thy correction hath wrought medicinally upon me, presume I upon that spirituall strength I have; but as I acknowledge, that my bodily strength is subiect to every puffe of wind, so is my spirituall strength to every blast of vanitie. Keepe me therefore still, O my gracious God, in such a proportion of both strengths, as I may still have something to thanke thee for, which I have received, and still something to pray for, and aske at thy hand.

🌿 The Prayers: Group 4 🌿

From the *LETTERS,* written at various times, published in
1633 ff.

A. *To the right wor. Sir Geo. More, kt.*
    Sir,
        The inward accusacions in my conscience, that I have
offended you beyond any ability of redeeming it by me, and the
feeling of my Lord's [Sir Thomas Egerton's] heavy displeasure
following it [my elopement with Anne More], forceth me to
wright, though I know my faults make my letters very ungraci-
ous to you. [May] Allmighty God, whom I call to witnesse that
all my griefe is that I have in this manner offended you and him,
direct you to beleeve that which owt of an humble and afflicted
h[e]art I now wright to you. And since we have no meanes to
move God, when he will not hear our prayers, to hear them,
but by prayeng, I humbly beseech you to allow by his gracious
example, my penitence so good entertainment, as it may have
a beeliefe and a pittie. ... And though perchance you intend not
utter destruction, yett the way through which I fall towards it is
so headlong, that beeing thus pushed, I shall soone be at bot-
tome, for it pleaseth God, from whom I acknowledge the punishment to be just, to accompany my other ills with so much sicknes as I have no refuge but that of mercy, which I beg of him,
my Lord, and you, which I hope you will not repent to have
afforded me. ... From the Fleete [Prison], 11 Febr. 1601 [/2].
        Yours in all faythfull duty and obedience,
                                        J. DONNE

The Prayers of John Donne

B. *To the right honorable my very good Lord and Master
Sir Thomas Egerton, knight, Lord Keeper of the Great
Seale of England.*

. . . The whole world is a streight imprisonment to me,
whilst I ame barr'd your Lordship's sight; but this favor [namely,
your granting me "liberty to take the ayre about this towne"]
may lengthen and better my lyfe, which I desire to preserve,
onely in hope to redeeme by my sorrowe and desire to do your
Lordship service, my offence past. [May] Allmighty God dwell
ever in your Lordship's h[e]art, and fill it with good desires,
and graunt them.

Your Lordship's poorest servant,

[*Early in* 1601 /2]   J. DONNE

C. *To his Mother: comforting her after the death of her
Daughter*   [1616]

. . . Joyne with God, and make his visitations and afflictions, as he intended them, mercies and comforts. And, for
God's sake, pardon those negligences, which I have heretofore
used towards you; and assist me, with your blessing to me,
and all mine; and with your prayers to our blessed Saviour, that
thereby both my mind and fortune, may be apt to do all my
duties, especially those that belong to you.

[May] God, whose omnipotent strength can change the nature of any thing, by his raising-Spirit of comfort, make your
Povertie Riches, your Afflictions Pleasure, and all the Gall and
Wormwood of your life, Hony and Manna to your taste, which
he hath wrought, whensoever you are willing to have it so.
Which, because I cannot doubt in you, I will forbear more lines
at this time, and most humblie deliver my self over to your devotions, and good opinion of me, which I desire no longer to
live, than I may have.

The Prayers: Group Four

D.   *To the R: Honorable Sir Thomas Roe, Ambassador for His Majestie of Great Britaine to the Grand Seignor.*

. . . [Our] B[lessed]: Savyor give you the comfort of it ["the delyveringe of a good opinion of you"] all your way, and the reward of it, at last. Many graines make up the bread that feeds us; and many thornes make up the Crown that must glorifie us; and one of those thornes is, for the most part, the stinginge calumny of others' tongues. . . . I recommend myselfe to your Lordship's prayers; and I enwrap you, with mine own soule in mine: and our B: God enwrap in the righteousnes of his sonne, both you and

Your Lordship's/humblest and thankfullest Servant in Christ Jesus.

J. DONNE

at my poore house at
St. Paul's, London 1° *Decemb.* 1622

E.   *To the Honourable L[ady], the Lady Kingsmel upon the death of her Husband*

. . . The difference is great in the loss, of an arme, or a head; of a child, or a husband: but to them, who are incorporated into Christ, their head, there can be no beheading; upon you, who are a member of the spouse of Christ the Church, there can fall no widowhead, nor orphanage upon those children, to whom God is father. I have not another office by your husband's death; for I was your Chaplaine before, in my daily prayers; but I shall inlarge that office with other Collects, than before, that God will continue to you, that peace which you have ever had in him, and send you quiet, and peaceable dispositions in all them with whom you shall have any thing to do, in your temporall estate and matters of this world. Amen.

75

Your Ladiship's very humble and/thankfull servant in Christ/Jesus.

At my poor house at S.
Paul's. 26 . Octob./1624

J. DONNE

F.   *To the honourable kt. and my most honoured friend Sir Henry Wotton, Provost of Eton*

. . . And for the favor which you shall be pleased to afford us herein ["about any place in your colledge"], I offer your mother and daughters, all the service I shall be able to doe to any servant of yours in any place of any of our churches. Our most B. Savyor blesse you with all his graces, and restore us to a confident meetinge in wholesome place, and direct us all by good ways to good ends. Amen.

Your very true fri[e]nde and humble/servant in Christ Jesus

J. DONNE

From Sir John Danvers' house at Chelsey . . .
12 Julli, 1625.

G.   *To [the Earl of Dorset ?]*

Our blessed Savyor establish in you, and multiply to you, the seals of his eternall election, and testify his gracious purposes towards you in the next world for ever, by a continuall succession of his outward blessings here, and sweeten your age, by a rectified conscience of havinge spent your former tyme well and sweeten your transmigration by a modest but yet infallible assurance of a present union with him. Amen. . . . Almighty God blesse you where you are, and where you would be, when you are there, and bringe you thether. Amen.

your Lordship's humblest and thankfullest/servant in Christ Jesus

At Chelsey.
25 November 1625

J. DONNE

The Prayers: *Group Four*

H.   *To the worthiest Knight Sir Henry Goodere.*
[21 December 1625]

Sir,

Our blessed Saviour, who abounds in power and goodnesse towards us all, blesse you, and your family, with blessings
proportioned to his ends in you all, and blesse you with the
testimony of a rectified conscience, of having discharged all the
offices of a father, towards your discreet and worthy daughters,
and blesse them with a satisfaction, and quiescence, and more,
with a complacency and a joy, in good ends, and ways towards
them, Amen. . . .

I.   [*To Mrs. Cokain*]

. . . In so noble and numerous a family as yours is, every
year must necessarily present you some such occasion of sorrow,
in the losse of some near friend. And therefore I, in the office
of a Friend, and a Brother, and Priest of God, do not onelie
look that you should take this [death of your son] patientlie,
as a declaration of God's present will; but that you take it cate-
chistically, as an instruction for the future; and that God, in
this, tells you, That he will do so again, in some other your
friends. For, to take any one crosse patiently, is but to forgive
God for once; but to surrender one's self entirely to God, is to
be ready for all that he shall be pleased to do. And, that his
pleasure may be either to lessen your crosses, or multiply your
strength, shall be the prayer of

Your Brother, and Friend, and/Servant, and Chaplain,
[1629]   JOHN DONNE

J.   *To my very much honoured friend George Garrard* [*Ger-
rard*] *Esquire at Sion*

. . . Our blessed Saviour multiply his blessings upon
that noble family where you are, and your self, and your sonne;

77

as upon all them that are derived from
Your poor friend and servant

J. DONNE

[*October,* 1630]

K.   *To my honoured friend G[eorge]. G[errard]. Esquire*

. . . But I do but discourse, I do not wish; life, or health, or strength, (I thank God) enter not into my prayers for my self: for others they do; and amongst others, for your sick servant, for such a servant taken so young, and healed [healthy] so long, is half a child to a master, and so truly I have observed that you have bred him, with the care of a father. Our blessed Saviour look graciously upon him, and glorifie himself in him, by his way of restitution to health; And by his way of peace of conscience in
Your very true friend and servant in Chr. Jes.

J. DONNE

[2 *November* 1630]

L.   *To my very much Honoured friend George Garret [Gerrard] Esquire*

. . . God blesse you and your sonne, with the same blessings which I begge for the children, and for the person of
Your poor friend and humble/servant in Chr. Jes.

J. DONNE

[*Abury Hatch, December,* 1630]

M.   *To The Honourable Companie of the Virginian Planta-*
     tion.   [1622]

By your Favours, I had some place amongst you, before: but now I am an Adventurer; if not to Virginia, yet for Virginia; for, every man, that Prints, Adventures. For the Preaching of this Sermon, I was but under your Invitation; my Time was mine owne, and my Med[i]tations mine owne: and I had beene excusable towards you, if I had turn'd that Time, and those Meditations, to God's service, in any other place. But for the Printing of this Sermon, I am not onely under your Invitation, but under your Commandement; for, after it was preached, it was not mine, but yours: And therefore, if I gave it at first, I doe but restore it now. The first was an act of Love; this, of Iustice; both which Vertues, Almightie God evermore promove and exalt in all your proceedings. Amen.

      Your humble Servant/in Christ Iesus

                      IOHN DONNE

✣ The Prayers: Group 5 ✣

From the *SERMONS,* preached at various times, published
in 1622 ff.

A. Forgive me O Lord, O Lord forgive me my sinnes, the
sinnes of my youth, and my present sinnes, the sinne that my
Parents cast upon me, Originall sinne, and the sinnes that I
cast upon my children, in an ill example; Actuall sinnes, sinnes
which are manifest to all the world, and sinnes which I have
so laboured to hide from the world, as that now they are hid
from mine own conscience, and mine own memory; Forgive me
my crying sins, and my whispering sins, sins of uncharitable
hate, and sinnes of unchaste love, sinnes against Thee and Thee,
against thy Power O Almighty Father, against thy Wisedome,
O glorious Sonne, against thy Goodnesse, O blessed Spirit of
God; and sinnes against Him and Him, against Superiours and
Equals, and Inferiours; and sinnes against Me and Me, against
mine own soul, and against my body, which I have loved better
than my soul; Forgive me O Lord, O Lord in the merits of thy
Christ and my Jesus, thine Anointed, and my Saviour; Forgive
me my sinnes, all my sinnes, and I will put Christ to no more
cost, nor thee to more trouble, for any reprobation or maledic-
tion that lay upon me, otherwise than as a sinner. I ask but an
application, not an extention of that Benediction, *Blessed are
they whose sinnes are forgiven;* Let me be but so blessed, and I
shall envy no man's Blessednesse: say thou to my sad soul, *Sonne
be of good comfort, thy sinnes are forgiven thee,* and I shall
never trouble thee with Petitions, to take any other Bill off of

81

The Prayers of John Donne

the fyle, or to reverse any other Decree, by which I should be accurst, before I was created, or condemned by thee, before thou saw'st me as a sinner.

B.   O Eternall, and most gracious God, Father of our Lord Iesus Christ; and in him, of all those that are his, As thou diddest make him so much ours, as that he became like us, in all things, sinne onely excepted, make us so much his, as that we may be like him, even without the exception of sinne, that all our sinnes may bee buryed in his wounds, and drowned in his Blood. And as this day wee celebrate his Ascension to thee, bee pleased to accept our endeavour of conforming our selves to his patterne, in raysing [raising] this place [a new chapel at Lincoln's Inn] for our Ascension to him. Leane upon these Pinnacles, O Lord, as thou diddist upon Iacob's Ladder, and hearken after us. Bee this thine Arke, and let thy Dove, thy blessed Spirit, come in and out, at these Windowes: and let a full pot of thy Manna, a good measure of thy Word, and an effectuall preaching thereof, bee evermore preserved, and evermore bee distributed in this place. Let the Leprosie of Superstition never enter within these Walles, nor the hand of Sacriledge ever fall upon them. And in these walles, to them that love Profit and Gaine, manifest thou thy selfe as a Treasure, and fill them so; To them that love Pleasure, manifest thy selfe, as Marrow and Fatnesse, and fill them so; And to them that love Preferment, manifest thy selfe, as a Kingdome, and fill them so; that so thou mayest bee all unto all; give thy selfe wholly to us all, and make us all wholly thine. Accept our humble thanks for all, etc.

C.   O Eternall, and most Glorious God, who sometimes in thy Iustice, dost give *the dead bodies of the Saints, to be meat unto the Fowles of the Heaven, and the flesh of thy Saints unto the beasts of the Earth* [margin: Psalm 79, 2], so that *their bloud is shed like water, and there is none to burie them,* Who

82

sometimes, *sel'st thy People for nought, and dost not increase thy wealth, by their price* [margin: Psalm 44, 12], and yet never leav'st us without that knowledge, That *precious in thy sight is the death of thy Saints* [margin: Psalm 116, 15], inable us, in life and death, seriously to consider the value, the price of a Soule. It is precious, O Lord, because thine Image is stampt, and imprinted upon it; Precious, because the bloud of thy Sonne was paid for it; Precious, because thy blessed Spirit, the Holy Ghost workes upon it, and tries it, by his divers fires; And precious, because it is enter'd into thy Revenue, and made a part of thy Treasure. Suffer us not therefore, O Lord, so to undervalue our selves, nay, so to impoverish thee, as to give away those soules, thy soules, thy deare and precious soules, for nothing, and all the world is nothing, if the Soule must be given for it. We know, O Lord, that our Rent, due to thee, is our Soule; and the day of our death, is the day, and our Deathbed the place, where this Rent is to bee paid. And wee know too, that hee that hath sold his soule before, for uniust gaine, or given away his soule before, in the society and fellowship of sinne, or lent away his soule, for a time, by a lukewarmnesse, and temporizing, to the dishonor of thy name, to the weak'ning of thy cause, to the discouraging of thy Servants, he comes to that day, and to that place, his Death, and Death-bed, without any Rent in his hand, without any soule, to this purpose, to surrender it unto thee. Let therefore O Lord, the same hand which is to receive them then, preserve these soules till then; Let that mouth, that breath'd them into us, at first, breath[e] alwaies upon them, whilst they are in us, and sucke them into it selfe, when they depart from us. Preserve our soules O Lord, because they belong to thee; and preserve our bodies, because they belong to those soules. Thou alone, dost steere our Boat, through all our Voyage, but hast a more especiall care of it, a more watchfull eye upon it, when it comes to a narrow currant, or to a dangerous fall of waters. Thou hast a care of the preservation of

these bodies, in all the waies of our life; But in the Straights of
Death, open thine eyes wider, and enlarge thy providence towards us, so farre, that no Fever in the body, may shake the
soule, no Apoplexie in the body, dampe or benumbe the soule,
nor any paine, or agonie of the body, presage future torments to
the soule. But so make thou our bed in all our sicknesse, that
being us'd to thy hand, wee may be content with any bed of thy
making; Whether thou bee pleas'd to change our feathers into
flockes, by withdrawing the conveniences of this life, or to change
our flockes into dust, even the dust of the Grave, by withdrawing
us out of this life. And though thou divide man and wife,
mother and child, friend and friend, by the hand of Death, yet
stay them that stay, and send them away that goe, with this consolation, that though we part at divers daies, and by divers
waies, here, yet wee shall all meet at one place, and at one day,
a day that no night shall determine, the day of the glorious
Resurrection. Hasten that day, O Lord, for their sakes, that beg
it at thy hands, from under the Altar in Heaven; Hasten it for
our sakes, that groane under the manifold incombrances of these
mortall bodies; Hasten it for her [the Lady Danvers'] sake,
whom wee have lately laid downe, in this thy holy ground; And
hasten it for thy Son Christ Iesus' sake, to whom then, and not
till then, all things shall bee absolutely subdu'd. Seale to our
soules now an assurance of thy gracious purpose towards us in
that day, by accepting this daie's service, at our hands. Accept our
humble thankes, for all thy benefits, spirituall, and temporall,
already bestowed upon us, and accept our humble prayers for
the continuance and enlargement of them. Continue, and enlarge
them, O God upon thine universall Church, dispersed, etc.

D.   But if, O Lord, I see these foundations destroyed [this
sermon's text is Psalm 11, 3: *If the foundations be destroyed,
what can the righteous do?*], if thou put mee into mine Enemies'
hand, if thou make them thy Sword, if their furie draw that

The Prayers: Group Five

Sword, and then, thy Almightie Arme, sinewed even with thine owne indignation, strike with that sword, what can I, how righteous soever I were, doe?

E.   Enlarge our daies, O Lord, to that blessed day [*the day of the Lord,* Amos 5, 18], prepare us before that day, seale to us at that day, ratifie to us after that day, all the daies of our life, an assurance in that Kingdome, which thy Son our Saviour hath purchased for us, with the inestimable price of his incorruptible bloud, To which glorious Son of God, etc.

F.   I offer not therefore at [my tongue or lips to express] it [the resurrection of the body]: but in respect of, and with relation to that blessed State, according to the doctrine, and practise of our Church, we doe pray for the dead; for the militant Church upon earth, and the triumphant Church in Heaven, and the whole Catholique Church in Heaven, and earth; we doe pray that God will be pleased to hasten that Kingdome, that we with all others departed in the true Faith of his holy Name, may have this perfect consummation, both of body and soule, in his everlasting glory, Amen.

G.   We returne to thee againe, O God, with praise and prayer; as for all thy mercies from before minutes began, to this minute, from our Election to this present beame of Sanctification which thou hast shed upon us now. And more particularly, that thou hast afforded us that great dignity, to be, this way witnesses of thy Sonne Christ Iesus, and instruments of his glory. Looke graciously, and looke powerfully upon this body, which thou hast bene now some yeares in building and compacting together, this [Honourable Company of the Virginian] Plantation. Looke graciously upon the Head of this Body, our Soveraigne, and blesse him with a good disposition to this work, and blesse him for that disposition: Looke gratiously upon them, who are as the braine of this body, those who by his power, counsell, and advise, and assist in the Government thereof: blesse them with disposition to unity and concord, and blesse them for that disposition: Looke gratiously upon them who are as Eyes of this Body, those of the Clergy, who have any interest therein: blesse them with a disposition to preach there, to pray heere, to exhort every where, for the advancement thereof, and bless them for that disposition. Blesse them who are the Feete of this body, who goe thither, and the Hands of this body, who labour there, and them who are the Heart of this bodie, all that are heartily affected, and declare actually that heartinesse to this action, blesse them all with a cheerefull disposition to that, and bless them for that disposition. Bless it so in this calme, that when the tempest comes, it may ride it out safely; blesse it so with friends now, that it may stand against Enemies hereafter; prepare thy selfe a glorious harvest there, and give us leave to be thy Labourers, That so the number of thy Saints being fulfilled, wee may with better assurance ioyne in that prayer, *Come Lord Iesus, come quickly,* and so meet all in that Kingdome which the Sonne of God hath purchased for us with the inestimable price of his incorruptible Bloud. To which glorious Sonne of God, etc. Amen.

H.   And what glory soever thou hast had in this world, Glory inherited from noble Ancestors, Glory acquired by merit and service, Glory purchased by money, and observation, what glory of beauty and proportion, what glory of health and strength soever thou hast had in this house of clay, *The glory of the lat[t]er house, shall be greater than of the former* [margin: Haggai 2, 9]. To this glory, the God of this glory, by glorious or inglorious waies, such as may most advance his own glory, bring us in his time, for his Son Christ Jesus' sake. Amen.

I.   Almighty God worke in you a perfit dedication of your selves at this time [the Feast of Dedication]; that so, receiving it from hands dedicated to God, hee whose holy Office this is, may present acceptably this House [a new chapel at Lincoln's Inn] to God in your behalfes, and establish an assurance to you, that God will be alwayes present with you and your Succession in this place. Amen.

J.   This constancy, and this ["true confidence proceeds onely out of true Goodnesse"] confidence, and upon this ground, Holy courage in a holy feare of him, Almighty God infuse and imprint in you all, for his Son Christ Jesus' sake. And to this glorious Son of God, etc.

K.   In the presence of God, we lay him [Sir William Cokayne, Knight, Alderman of London] downe; In the power of God, he shall rise; In the person of Christ, he is risen already. And so into the same hands that have received his soule, we commend his body; beseeching his blessed Spirit, that as our charity enclines us to hope confidently of his good estate, our faith may assure us of the same happinesse, in our owne behalfe; And that for all our sakes, but especially for his own glory, he will be pleased to hasten the consummation of all, in that kingdome which that Son of God hath purchased for us, with the inestimable price of his incorruptible blood. Amen.

L.   Almighty God inform us, and reveale unto us, what this *Better Resurrection* [of this sermon's text, Hebrews 11, 35] is, by possessing us of it; And make the hastening to it, one degree of addition in it. *Come Lord Jesus, come quickly* to the consummation of that Kingdome which thou hast purchased for us, with inestimable price of thine incorruptible blood. Amen.

M.   That God that is the God of peace, grant us his peace, and one minde towards one another; That God that is the Lord of Hosts, maintaine in us that warre, which himself hath proclaimed, an enmity between the seed of the Woman, and the seed of the Serpent, between the truth of God, and the inventions of men; That we may fight his battels against his enemies without, and fight his battels against our enemies within, our own corrupt affections; That we may be victorious here, in our selves, and over our selves, and triumph with him hereafter, in eternall glory.

N.   *The key of David opens, and no man shuts.* The Son of David, is the key of David, Christ Jesus; He hath opened heaven for us all; let no man shut out himself, by diffidence in God's mercy, nor shut out any other man, by overvaluing his own purity, in respect of others. But forbearing all lacerations, and tearings, and woundings of one another, with bitter invectives, all exasperations by odious names of subdivision, let us all study, first the redintegration of that body, of which Christ Jesus hath declared himselfe to be the head, the whole Christian Church, and pray that he would, and hope that he will enlarge the means of salvation to those, who have not yet been made partakers of it. That so, he that called the gates of heaven straite, may say to those gates, *Elevamini portae aeternales, Be ye lifted up, ye eternall gates* [margin: Psalm 24, 7], and be ye enlarged, that as the King of glory himself is ent'red into you, for the farther glory of the King of glory, not only that hundred and foure and forty thousand of the Tribes of the children of Israel, but that multitude which is spoken of in that place [margin: Apoc. 7, 19, but should be 7, 9], *which no man can number, of all Nations, and Kindreds, and People,* and friends, may enter with that acclamation, Salvation to our God, which sitteth upon the Throne, and to the Lamb for ever. And unto this City of the living *God,* the heavenly Ierusalem, and to the innumerable company of Angels, to the generall assembly, and Church of the first born, which are written in heaven, and to *God* the Iudge of all, and to the spirits of just men made perfect, and to Iesus the Mediator of the new covenant, and to the blood of sprinkling, that speaks better things than that of Abel [margin: Hebrews 12, 22 to 24], Blessed God bring us all, for thy Son's sake, and by the operation of thy Spirit. Amen.

O.   Lighten our darknesse, we beseech thee, O Lord, that *in thy light we may see light*: illustrate our understandings, kindle our affections, poure oyl to our zeal, that we may come to the marriage of this Lambe [in the text, Hosea 2, 19], and that this Lambe may come quickly to this marriage: and in the mean time blesse these thy servants, with making this secular marriage a type of the spirituall, and the spirituall an earnest of that eternall, which they and we by thy mercie shall have in that kingdome, which thy Sonne our Saviour hath purchased with the inestimable price of his incorruptible bloud. To whom, etc.

P.   There ["as God breathed a soule into the first Adam, so this second Adam breathed his soule into God, into the hands of God"] wee leave you, in that blessed dependancy, to hang upon him that hangs upon the Crosse, there bath[e] in his teares, there suck at his woundes, and lye downe in peace in his grave, till hee vouchsafe you a resurrection, and an ascension into that Kingdome, which hee hath prepared for you, with the inestimable price of his incorruptible blood. Amen.

🎗 The Prayers: Group 6 🎗

Miscellaneous

A. From Donne's private account book kept when dean:

1624/1625. *Deo Opt. Max. benigno Largitori, à me, et ab iis quibus haec à me reservantur, gloria, et gratia in aeternum. Amen.*

1626. *Multiplicatae sunt super nos misericordiae tuae Domine. Da Domine, ut quae ex immensa bonitate tua nobis elargiri dignatus sis, in quorum cunque manus devenerint, in tuam semper cedant gloriam. Amen.*

1628. *In fine horum sex annorum manet.* [. . .]

1629. *Quid habeo, quod non accepi à Domino? Largiatur etiam, ut quae largitus est, sua iterum fiant bono eorum usu, ut quemadmodum, nec officiis hujus mundi, nec loci, in quo me posuit, dignitati, nec servis, nec egenis, in toto hujus anni curriculo, mihi conscius sum, me defuisse, ita ut liberi, quibus quae supersunt, supersunt, grato animo ea accipiant, et beneficum Authorem recognoscant. Amen.*

B. Translated out of Gazaeus, *Vota Amico Facta*:

God grant thee thine own wish, and grant thee mine,
Thou, who dost, best friend, in best things outshine;
May thy soul, ever chearfull, ne're know cares,
Nor thy life, ever lively, know gray haires.
Nor thy hand, ever open, know base holds,
Nor thy purse, ever plump, know pleits, or folds.

Nor thy tongue, ever true, know a false thing,
Nor thy word, ever mild, know quarrelling.
Nor thy works, ever equall, know disguise,
Nor thy fame, ever pure, know contumelies.
  Nor thy prayers, know low objects, still Divine;
God grant thee thine own wish, and grant thee mine.

C.   From Donne's will:

In the name of the blessed and glorious Trinitie, Amen.
I Iohn Donne, by the mercy of Christ Iesus, and [by] the calling
of the Church of England, Priest, being at this time in good
[health?]and perfect understanding, (praised be God therefore)
doe hereby make my last Will and Testament in manner and
forme following.

First, I give my gracious God an intire sacrifice of body
and soule, with my most humble thanks for that assurance which
his blessed Spirit imprints in me now of the salvation of the
one, and of the resurrection of the other; And for that constant
and cheerfull resolution which the same Spirit [hath] established in me, to live and die in the Religion now professed in
the Church of England: In expectation of that Resurrection I
desire my body may be buried (in the most private manner that
may be) in that place of S[t]. Paul's Church London, that the
now Residentiaries have at my request assigned for that purpose,
etc. . . .

And this my last Will and Testament made in the feare of
God, (whose merit I humbly beg, and constantly rely upon in
Iesus Christ) and in perfect love and charity with all the world,
whose pardon I aske from the lowest of my servants to the
highest of my Superiours. Written all with mine owne hand,
and my name subscribed to every Page, being five in number.

Notes:
Textual and Explanatory

As will be seen, these notes refer principally to earliest sources. Most useful of modern editions, biographies, and commentaries are:

A BIBLIOGRAPHY OF DR. JOHN DONNE, by Geoffrey Keynes, 2nd. edition, Cambridge, 1932

JOHN DONNE SINCE 1900: *A BIBLIOGRAPHY OF PERIOD-ICAL ARTICLES,* by William White, Boston, 1942

THE POEMS OF JOHN DONNE, edited from the old editions and numerous manuscripts, with introductions and commentary, by Herbert J. C. Grierson, 2 volumes, Oxford, 1912

JOHN DONNE: COMPLETE POETRY AND SELECTED PROSE, edited by John Hayward, London, 1929

A STUDY OF THE PROSE WORKS OF JOHN DONNE, by Mrs. E. M. Simpson, 2nd. edition, Oxford, 1948

THE LIFE AND LETTERS OF JOHN DONNE, NOW FOR THE FIRST TIME REVISED AND COLLECTED, by Edmund Gosse, 2 volumes, London, 1899

These helps will be referred to by editor's name only. The as yet unpublished biography by R. C. Bald, and the forthcoming edition of the sermons by G. R. Potter and Mrs. E. M. Simpson, should be valuable.

On the general subject of Christian prayer, worth recommending here is the practical and thorough analysis by the Rev. Erwin T. Umbach, printed in *Proceedings of the 29th. Convention of the Atlantic District of The Lutheran Church—Missouri Synod,* 1949, pp. 22 to 43.

With pleasure and respect I acknowledge indebtedness to the resources of especially The Folger Shakespeare Library and The Library
of Congress. Their manuscripts, original editions, and other primary
source materials are the very heart of this my edition.

Though the purpose of this anthology is that of making Donne's
written prayers available to modern readers, and is therefore not
merely antiquarian, it has seemed to me best nevertheless to retain
the peculiarities of the original spelling and punctuation. These inevitably will bring the reader closer to the Renaissance practice. Likewise I have retained the custom of both Donne and his printers in
using the capital and small initial letters freely. The numerous
rhetorical pauses, for which Donne used many commas, are useful
in devotional writing.

For clarity, however, in a collection drawn from various early
sources and intended to be reasonably easy to read today, I have
made the following editorial changes consistently:

a) interchanged letters u and v are brought into accord with
   modern usage, and long s is printed in modern style;
b) "then" in the sense of today's "than" regularly uses the a form;
c) possessive case endings are indicated by the inserted apostrophe,
   as are contractions used in the original;
d) superabundance of italicized words and phrases is reduced by
   restricting italics chiefly to some direct Bible quotations and
   Latin or other foreign terms;
e) the irregularly employed ampersand & is replaced by con-
   ventional "and" or "etc." as the context requires.

Incidental typographical or other little errors are corrected in the text
by bracketed inserts. Some abbreviations are similarly expanded.

Obviously the many passages which loosely use the word "pray"
(e. g. in a letter Donne says: "Keep it [a copy of *Biathanatos*], I
pray, with the same jealousy") are not our concern in this book.

THE INTRODUCTION

1. *LXXX Sermons* . . . 1640 (hereafter designated *LXXX*), #59,
   p. 592, "Preached upon the Penitentiall Psalmes," the fifth sentence in the opening paragraph. Text: Psalm 32, 6.

Notes: Textual and Explanatory

2. *LXXX,* #80, p. 820, "Preached at the funerals of Sir William Cokayne, Knight[,] Alderman of London, December 12. 1626." Text: John 11, 21.

3. *Letters to Severall Persons of Honour . . .* 1651 (hereafter designated *Letters*), p. 49, "To Sir H[enry] Goodere," Sept. 1608. The word *inhiation* is defined in the *New English Dictionary on Historical Principles* (hereafter designated *N.E.D.*) as "the act of gaping after, or desiring greedily," in illustration whereof this Donne passage is printed.

4. *Poems . . .,* ed. Grierson (hereafter designated Grierson), Vol. I, p. 331, "Divine Poems," #19. The word *humorous* is here technical, in the *N.E.D.* sense of "subject to, influenced by, or dependent on humour or mood; full of humours or fancies; fanciful, capricious, whimsical".

5. *LXXX,* #13, p. 130, "Preached in Lent, To the King. April 20. 1630." Text: Job 16, 17 to 19.

6. *LXXX,* #45, pp. 452 and 453, "Preached upon All-Saints Day." Text: Apoc. 7, 2 and 3. The context aptly says: "None of us hath got the victory over flesh and blood, and yet we have greater enemies than flesh and blood are."

7. *Fifty Sermons . . .* 1649 (hereafter designated *Fifty*), #11, p. 88, "Preached at Lincoln's Inne, preparing them to build their Chappell."

8. *LXXX,* #80 (see fn. 2), pp. 819 and 820. The word *evacuated* here means "to make void, annul, deprive of force or validity. Chiefly in religious and legal phraseology" (*N.E.D.*).

9. Notice the analogies from literature. I have not been able to identify the actual primary source in Donne, so I give it as quoted from Donne in *The Dogmatic and Mystical Theology of John Donne* by Itrat Husain, London, 1938, p. 123.

10. *LXXX,* #80 (see fn. 2), pp. 822 and 823. The building metaphor is beautifully used in the opening words of *Death's Duell.*

11. *Letters,* pp. 111 and 112, "To S[i]r H[enry] G[oodyer]" in 1609. In another letter to the same correspondent while discussing religion, April 1615 (p. 101), Donne used the phrases "the inobedient Puritans, and . . . the over-obedient Papists." In *A Collection of Letters, made by S[i]r Tobie Mathews . . .*1660 (hereafter designated Tobie Mathews), p. 337, "A Letter of much kindnesse from Doctor Donne, to Sir Toby Mathew, from Col-

leyn" in 1619 says: "That which I add, I am farre from applying to you, but it is true, That we are fallen into so slack and negligent times, that I have been sometimes glad to hear, that some of my friends have differed from me in Religion. It is some degree of an union to be united in a serious meditation of God, and to make any Religion the rule of our actions. Our sweet and blessed Saviour bring us by his way, to his end!" Interesting in this connection is Problem 2 in Donne's *Iuvenilia: or certaine Paradoxes, and Problemes . . .* 1633, entitled "Why Puritans make long Sermons."

12. *LXXX,* #9, p. 90, "Preached upon Candlemas day." Text: Romans 13, 7, "The Text being part of the Epistle of that day, that yeare." The preceding context uses this metaphysical figure: "And for the debt of prayer, God will not be paid, with money of our owne coyning, (with sudden, extemporall, inconsiderate prayer) but with currant money, that beares the King's Image, and inscription; The Church of God, by his Ordinance, hath set his stampe, upon a Liturgie and Service, for his house." The later, expanded editions of Walton's *Lives . . .* record such ejaculations of Donne that are like prayers, as Donne used them after the death of his wife.

13. *LXXX,* #76, p. 768, "Preached to the Earle of Carlile, and his Company, at Sion." Text: Mark 16, 16. The word *deprehend,* as the *N.E.D.* quotes from another of Donne's sermons, here means "to catch or detect (a person) in the commission of some evil or secret deed; to take by surprise". In *Fifty,* #27, p. 230, "Preached to the King at White-hall the First of April 1627," Donne said: "And even Nature it self taught the naturall man, to make that one argument of a man truly religious, *Aperto vivere voto,* That he durst pray aloud, and let the world heare, what he asked at God's hand; which duty is best performed, when we joyne with the Congregation in publique prayer."

14. *LXXX,* #4, p. 35, "Preached at S[t]. Paul's upon Christmas Day. 1626." Text: Luke 2, 29 and 30. The phrase "cock of water" near the end of my quotation may be emended to read "crock of water," but the original has good meaning in a technical application of "a spout or short pipe serving as a channel for passing liquids through, and having an appliance for regulating or stopping the flow; a tap" (*N.E.D.*).

15. *LXXX,* #2, p. 12, "Preached at Paul's upon Christmas Day,

96

Notes: Textual and Explanatory

in the Evening. 1624." Text: Esaiah 7, 14, which was "Part of the first lesson, that Evening."

16. *Fifty,* #40, p. 366, "Preached at Saint Paul's." A verse-letter "To Sir Henry Goodyere" (Grierson, Vol. I, p. 184, lines 37 to 40) phrases the need of such a "right way of reconciliation to God" thusly:

> However, keepe the lively tast[e] you hold
> Of God, love him as now, but feare him more,
> And in your afternoones thinke what you told
> And promis'd him, at morning prayer before.

17. *LXXX,* #4 (see fn. 14), pp. 35 and 36. The ending of *LXXX,* #58, p. 592, uses the same triad: ". . . in prayer, in preaching, in the Sacrament. For this is thy trinity upon earth, that must bring thee to the Trinity in heaven."

18. See group 1, secton R, where this poem is given in full.

19. *LXXX,* #52, p. 529, "Preached upon the Penitentiall Psalmes." Text: Psalm 6, 4 and 5.

20. *LXXX,* #50, p. 503, "Preached upon the Penitentiall Psalmes." Text: Psalm 6, 1.

21. "Letter to the Prince of [Wales]" in 1610, as printed in Hayward, p. 462 (not included in Gosse). The book *Pseudo-Martyr* to which Donne refers, dedicated to King James I, was the first controversial work by him to be printed.

22. *The First Sermon preached to King Charles . . . ,* original edition 1625, pp. 56 and 57. See group 5, section D.

23. *LXXX,* #80 (see fn. 2), p. 822. Sometimes Donne himself used prayer generalizations for others: e. g. " . . . because not knowing what seasons of weather are best for your use of the Bath, I know not what weather to pray for. I determine my prayers therefore in those Generalls, that God will give you whatsoever you would have, and multiplie it to you when you have it." (In "A Letter of much kindnesse from Doctor Donne, to the same friend [Mrs. Cokayne]," May, 1628. Tobie Mathews, p. 340.)

24. *Fifty,* #34, pp. 304 to 307.

25. *LXXX,* #52 (see fn. 19), p. 522. I have omitted only "The whole Psalme is Prayer; and" from this, the opening words of this sermon.

26. *XXVI Sermons . . .* 1660 (hereafter designated *XXVI*), #3, p. 31.

The Prayers of John Donne

27. *The Lives of Dr. John Donne, Sir Henry Wotton, Mr. Richard Hooker, Mr. George Herbert,* written by Izaak Walton, London, 1670, p. 80.

28. *The Life and Death of Dr. Donne, Late Dean of St. Paul's London,* prefixed to *LXXX,* sig. B 5 recto.

29. *LXXX,* #76 (see fn. 13), p. 767.

30. *LXXX,* #79, pp. 804 and 805, "Preached at S[t]. Paul's." Text: Psalm 90, 14.

31. *Fifty,* #43, p. 406, "A Sermon upon the fift[h] of Novemb[er]. 1622. being the Anniversary celebration.of our Deliverance from the [Gun]Powder Treason. Intended for Paul's Crosse, but by reason of the weather, Preached in the Church." *The Court and Times of James the First,* Vol. I, p. 300 ff. reveals that when negotiations were under way for the Spanish Marriage, James I released from prison a large number of Roman Catholics and thus stimulated rumors that the King intended to change his religion. In *Letters,* pp. 231 and 232, "To Sir H. G." Donne writes: ". . . they [as great a congr[egation] as ever I saw together, at Paul's Cross] received comfortable assurance of his Ma[jes]tie's constancy in Religion, and of his desire that all men should be bred in the knowledge of such things, as might preserve them from the superstition of Rome."

32. *Lives . . . ,* ed. 1670 (see fn. 27), p. 55. See group 1, section U.

33. *Letters,* p. 26.

34. *A Sermon upon the ninth Verse of the thirty-eighth Psalm . . . ,* facsimile ed. privately printed by Wilfred Merton from the Dowden Ms., London, 1921, (penciled) p. 152. George R. Potter has modernized this sermon in his edition called *A Sermon Preached at Lincoln's Inn . . . ,* Stanford, 1946, from which (p. 28) I include the phrase I placed in brackets.

35. Grierson, Vol. I, p. 197, "Letters to Severall Personages," lines 43 to 48. This poem is labeled "To the Countesse of Bedford, III" in the system used in *A Concordance to the English Poems of John Donne* by Combs and Sullens.

36. *A Sermon upon the ninth Verse of the thirty-eighth Psalm . . .* (See fn. 34), facsimile ed. pp. 159 and 160, or Potter's ed. pp. 33 and 34.

37. *LXXX,* #79 (see fn. 30), p. 810.

38. *Letters,* p. 111. See fn. 11. The word *seposed* means "to set apart

or reserve." The *N.E.D.* quotes this passage as an illustration. Mrs. Simpson, p. 93 fn. intelligently suggests for Donne's phrase "a type of the whole year in a Lent" the wording "a tithe" etc. The preceding context of Donne's letter says significantly: "And that advantage of nearer familiarity with God, which the act of incarnation gave us, is grounded upon God's assuming us, not our going to him."

39. *LXXX*, #59 (see fn. 1), p. 596. A 1612 letter to Sir Henry Wotton (Gosse, Vol. I, p. 293) refers to Donne's previous visit to France during the lifetime of Henry IV.

40. *LXXX*, #80 (see fn. 2), p. 820. Donne's polemical practice in his sermons throughout his ministry was in accord with instructions from "The Archbishop of Canterbury to the Bishops concerning King James his Directions for Preachers, with the Directions, Aug. 14, 1622," especially the fifth point:

> That no Preacher of what title or denomination soever shall causelessly or without invitation of the Text fall into bitter invectives, or undecent railing speeches against the persons of either Papists or Puritans; but modestly and gravely when they are occasioned thereunto by the text of Scripture, cleer both the doctrine and discipline of the Church of England from the aspersions of either adversary, especially when the Auditory is suspected with the one or the other infection.

(From *Scrinia Sacra; Secrets of Empire, in Letters of illustrious Persons.* A supplement of the *Cabala, Mysteries of State,* in letters of the great Ministers of K. James and K. Charles, London, 1654, p. 185.)

41. *Life* . . . (see fn. 28), sig. A 6 recto.

42. *Life* . . . (see fn. 28), sig. B 5 verso. Tobie Mathews, pp. 338 and 339, includes a letter of "Doctor Donne to Mrs. Cockaine, occasioned by the report of his death": "If you have believed the report, and mourned for me, I pray let that that is done alreadie, serve at the time that it shall be true. To mourn a second time, were to suspect that I were fallen into the second death, from which, I have abundant assurance, in the application of the superabundant Merits of my Saviour."

43. "A Letter between the same Persons," Tobie Mathews, p. 351.

44. *Letters,* pp. 36 and 37, "To Sir H. G." A decade earlier he wrote similarly, e. g. p. 159, "To the Honourable Knight Sir H. Goodere"

under date of Aug. 30, 1611: "Sir, I shall recompense my tedious-
nesse, in closing mine eyes with a prayer for yours, as for mine
own happinesse."
45. Grierson, Vol. I, p. 400. The English translation given by Walton,
   Life . . . (see fn. 28) translates a little differently:
       Under that little Seal great gifts I send
       Both works and pray'rs, pawns and fruits of a friend.
   The Latin is: *Mitto nec exigua, exiguâ sub imagine, dona,*
                 Pignora amicitiae, et munera; Vota, preces.
46. *Life* . . . (see fn. 28), sig. B 6 recto. Tobie Mathews, pp. 298
   and 299, prints an interesting exchange of letters between Donne
   and "the Queen of Bohemia, upon presenting of a Sermon to her"
   in 1626, in which this very friendly relationship can be glimpsed.
47. *LXXX,* #13 (see fn. 5), pp. 129 and 130. In the *Letters,* p. 181,
   "To my worthy friend G. K. Jan. 19" in 1613 Donne writes
   humorously: "I see not how I can admit that circuit of sending
   them [my rimes] to you, to be sent hither; that seems a kind
   of praying to Saints, to whom God must tell first, that such a
   man prays to them to pray to him."
48. *Letters,* p. 15, "To my honoured friend S[i]r. T[homas] Lucey.
   From Micham, my close prison ever since I saw you, 9 Octob." in
   1607.
49. *LXXX,* #25, p. 247, "Preached at S[t]. Paul's, upon Easter-day.
   1630." Text: Matthew 28, 6.
50. *The First Sermon preached to King Charles* . . . (see fn. 22), pp.
   2 and 3.
51. *LXXX,* #9 (see fn. 12), p. 90. The preceding context effectively
   states: "This is then our first debt to God, glory and praise. . . .
   Our other debt to God is Prayer, for that also is due to him, and
   him onely; For, *Si quod petendum est petis, sed non à quo
   petendum est, impius es* [margin: Augustine]: If we direct our
   prayers to any, even for temporall things, as to the Authors of
   those benefits, we may poure out as many prayers, as would have
   paid that debt, if they had been rightly placed, but yet by such a
   paiment, our debt is growne a debt of a higher nature, a sin."
52. *LXXX,* #79 (see fn. 30), p. 808.
53. LXXX, #9 (see fn. 12), p. 89. The subsequent context has this
   interesting antithesis: "When we meet in God's house, though, by
   occasion, there be no Sermon, yet if we meet to pray, we pay our

debt, we doe our duty; so doe we not, if we meet at a Sermon, without prayer."

54. *Letters*, pp. 160 and 164, "To his honourable friend S[i]r. H. G."

55. *Letters*, pp. 136 and 137, "To Sir H[enry] Wotton. Octob. the 4th. 1622. almost ad [at] midnight."

56. *LXXX*, #28, p. 281, "Preached at S[t]. Paul's, upon Whitsunday. 1627." Text: John 14, 26.

57. *A Sermon upon the ninth Verse of the thirty-eighth Psalm . . .* (see fn. 34), facsimile ed. p. 176, or Potter's ed. pp. 47 and 48. The deletion marks indicate a cross-out in the original, which Potter fills in from another ms.

58. *Letters*, pp. 209 and 210, dated December 22, 1607.

59. *Letters*, pp. 8 and 9. See group 4, section E. Without the second and third sentences, it is also in Tobie Mathews, p. 107, "Doctor Dunne writes Consolatorily to a Lady, upon the death of her Husband."

60. Tobie Mathews (see fn. 11), pp. 347 to 349, "A Letter from the aforesaid Doctor Donne to the same friend, occasioned by the death of her son." See group 4, section I.

61. Tobie Mathews, pp. 343 and 344, "A Letter between the same Persons," Donne and Mrs. Cokain.

62. *Fifty*, #14, p. 115, "Preached at Lincoln's Inne." Text: Job 19, 26.

63. *Life* . . . (see fn. 28), sig. B 6 verso.

64. *Death's Duell, or A Consolation to the Soule, against the dying Life, and living Death of the Body* . . . (see group 5, section P), original edition 1632, pp. 37 to 39. Reprinted with slight variations as the last sermon in *XXVI*. Text: Psalm 68, 20. The word *prolixious* means "long in extent or duration," and *dispositively* means "by way of or in regard to disposition, inclination, or tendency; opposed to effectively, actually; sometimes nearly=potentially" (*N.E.D.*, which quotes this passage as an illustration).

65. Grierson, Vol. I, p. 328, Holy Sonnet #13.

66. Grierson, Vol. I, p. 216, lines 37 to 40. Similarly Donne wrote "To my much honoured friend S[i]r. T[homas] Lu[e]y," August 16, 1622, from overseas: "Sir, our greatest business is more in our power than the least, and we may be surer to meet in heaven than in any place upon earth; and whilst we are distant here, we may meet as often as we list in God's presence, by soliciting in our prayers for one another." *Letters*, p. 188.

67. *LXXX*, #25, p. 253, "Preached at S[t]. Paul's, upon Easter-day. 1630," the conclusion of this sermon. Text: Matthew 28, 6. See group 5, section E ff.

THE SELECTED PRAYERS

GROUP 1: from *DIVINE POEMS*. Unmatched in their spiritual appeal, these religious poems are, together with the *Songs and Sonets* of his earlier days, Donne's best poems. Here is an effective combination of the talents of poet and divine. Some of this poetry was written before and some after he took orders; composed after 1610, published 1633 ff. My text and sequence are, with permission, from Grierson's definitive edition based on the early sources (which I have studied independently). To indicate metrical elision, I use the apostrophe without spacing, as is done in Grierson and Hayward.

A. The introductory sonnet to *La Corona*, a closely-woven sonnet-sequence of 7 poems with linking first and last lines. After this one, the topics are: "Annunciation," "Nativitie," "Temple," "Crucifying," "Resurrection," and the next (*Poems,* ed. Grierson, Vol. I. p. 318).

B. "Ascension," concluding sonnet of *La Corona* (I, 321).

C. The first of the *Holy Sonnets,* a series not as intricately interwoven as *La Corona* but more directly related in idea (I, 322). Included in the total 19, all without sub-titles, are the incomparable "Death be not proud" #10, and "I am a little world made cunningly" #5.

D. The second of the *Holy Sonnets* (I, 322).

E. The seventh ditto. (I, 325)

F. The fourteenth ditto (I, 328). This is an outstanding self-revelation.

G. The sixteenth ditto (I, 329).

H. The seventeenth ditto (I, 330). The death of his wife on August 15, 1617, is the central influence besides love of his Savior in Donne's later saintliness.

I. *Goodfriday, 1613. Riding Westward,* a short poem of 42 lines, of which these are 13 to 18 plus 33 to the end (I, 336 and 337).

J. Sub-titled "The Father," this is the opening stanza of *The Litanie,* a formal collect in 28 stanzas that vary in meter (I, 338). Only the first 13 have sub-titles. In a letter written apparently in 1610 "To Sir

Notes: Textual and Explanatory

H[enry] G[oodyer]," Donne wrote: "Since my imprisonment in my bed, I have made a meditation in verse, which I call a Litany; the word you know imports no other than supplication, but all Churches have one forme of supplication, by that name." (*Letters*, p. 32).

K. "The Sonne," the second stanza of *The Litanie* (I, 338).

L. "The Holy Ghost," the third ditto (I, 338 and 339).

M. "The Trinity," the fourth ditto (I, 339).

N. The twenty-third stanza ditto (I, 346).

O. The twenty-fourth ditto (I, 346).

P. The final stanza ditto (I, 348).

Q. *Upon the translation of the Psalmes by Sir Philip Sydney, and the Countesse of Pembroke his Sister,* called in line 45 "this Moses and this Miriam". These are the opening 16 lines of a 56 line poem of compliment to these famous literary contemporaries, with the concluding 8 lines (I, 348 to 350).

R. The complete 4 stanzas of *A Hymne to Christ, at the Author's last going into Germany* (I, 352 and 353). See Introduction, fn. 18, and this edition's keynote quotation from *XXVI*, #19, p. 280.

S. *The Lamentations of Ieremy, for the most part according to Tremelius.* This verse paraphrase is labored and stiff, but I include selections from chapters 3 (verses 1 and 20 to 26) and 5 (verses 1 and 16 to 22) to represent also this aspect of Donne's prayers (I, 360, 361, 366, and 367). Emanuel Tremellius (1510-'80) was a celebrated Hebrew scholar whose famous work was the Latin translation of the Old Testament completed in 1579 .

T. The complete 6 stanzas of the *Hymne to God My God, in my sicknesse,* composed 8 days before Donne's death (I, 368 and 369). In the fifth stanza "Adam's tree" is a reference to the Tree of the Knowledge of Good and Evil.

U. The complete 3 stanzas of *A Hymne to God the Father,* possibly the most intimate of Donne's prayers. I use Grierson's version (I, 369) rather than Walton's in the short *Life* . . . prefixed to *LXXX,* for uniformity in this group. Hayward prints this poem a little differently. Another version with the title *To Christ* and the final line "I have noe more" is printed in Grierson I, 370; also in II, 252 to 254, the music for this solemn hymn. An echo of the thought in the second stanza is found in a sermon on Matthew 21, 44 (*Fifty,* #35, p. 319): "There shall fall upon him [the sinner] those sinnes which he hath done after another's dehortation, and those, which others have done after his provocation."

GROUP 2: from *ESSAYES IN DIVINITY*. This, the least reprinted of our author's many writings, is sub-titled "Being Several Disquisitions, interwoven with Meditations and Prayers: Before he ent'red into Holy Orders." Composed about 1615, these essays were published by his son in 1651, whose preface asserts "that they were the voluntary sacrifices of severall hours, when he had many debates betwixt God and himself, whether he were worthy, and competently learned to enter into Holy Orders." I agree with Keynes, p. 76, in calling these expositions "a genuine record of their author's uncertainties in his transition from a lay to a clerical life. The four prayers with which the volume ends have a more obvious emotional and biographical value than the *Essayes* themselves."

A. This incidental prayer is found on pp. 26 to 29 in the original edition, where a quotation mark begins (but does not end) each line. The general topic under discussion is "Of Genesis", and in particular Part 1, "In the beginning." I omit 2 short portions that seem to ramble.

B. Included in the body of these essays, pp. 76 to 80, this prayer concludes the discussion of Genesis. Its learned style is more for display than devotion.

C. This and the next 3 prayers are grouped in the appendix, pp. 214 to 224. I think the notation in Walton's copy incorrect in saying Donne used these prayers before his sermons. Specifically, this one is abundantly full of contrition.

D. Mercy and justice are here balanced in more than a literary antithesis.

E. Effectively phrased here is a sincere renunciation of the world.

F. Refreshingly different here is the plea for mercy so that sometimes we humans may become angels.

GROUP 3: from *DEVOTIONS UPON EMERGENT OCCASIONS*. Written during a serious illness in 1623, 6 years after the death of his wife, Donne gave this book a significantly detailed title which continues: . . . *and severall steps in my Sicknes*. Digested into 1. Meditations

Notes: Textual and Explanatory

upon our Humane [Human] Conditions. 2. Expostulations, and Debatements with God. 3. Prayers, upon the severall Occasions, to him. . . . 1624. The prayers should be read not only in the entire context of the book, as a psychological case-history, but especially of the integrated triple division of each of the 23 total units. Here Donne is not concerned over others; instead, he is keenly sensitive about the state of his own repentant soul. Hopeful submission to God's will is prominent, with an occasional note of perplexity. Each unit is headed by a Latin tag with English translation, and all together are labeled *Stationes, sive Periodi in Morbo, ad quae referuntur Meditationes sequentes.*

A. From unit 1, "*Insultus Morbi primus.* The first alteration, The first grudging of the sicknesse," pp. 16 to 21. The metaphor of the circle is Donne's favorite figure of speech. At the end of the first paragraph "*shall spriug foorth*" is an obvious mis-print for "*shall spring foorth*," so I have emended it without special indication.

B. From unit 5, "*Solus adest.* The Phisician comes," pp. 110 to 115. Here too I have emended without special indication a typographical error near beginning, "*a Helpr fiet*" into a "a Helper fit" (italics omitted).

C. From unit 6, "*Metuit.* The Phisician is afraid," pp. 140 to 144. Memorable here is the exposition of the value of fear.

D. From unit 8, *Et Rex ipse suum mittit.* The King sends his owne Phisician," pp. 195 to 200. Unbounded gratitude to God is here emphasized.

E. From unit 9, "*Medicamina scribŭ[n]t.* Upon their [the physicians'] consulation, they prescribe," pp. 221 to 226.

F. From unit 15, "*Intereà insomnes noctes Ego duco, Diesque.* I sleepe not day nor night," pp. 382 to 387. The word *defensatives* means defensives, "something that serves to defend or protect; esp. in *Med.* and *Surg.* a bandage, plaster, ointment, or medicine, serving to guard against injury, inflammation, corruption, infection, etc." (*N.E.D.*).

G. From unit 17, "*Nunc lento sonitu dicunt, Morieris.* Now, this Bell tolling softly for another, saies to me, Thou must die," pp. 428 to 435. The now popular line, "and therefore never send to know for whom the bell tolls; it tolls for thee" is in the Meditation section of this unit (and in spirit in unit 16).

H. From unit 21, "*Atque annuit Ille, Qui, per eos, clamat, Linquas jam, Lazare, lectum.* God prospers their [the physicians'] practise, and he, by them, calls Lazarus out of his tombe, mee out of my bed," pp. 562 to 568.

GROUP 4: from the *LETTERS*. In this group more of the context needs to be given for prayer clarity. Published 1633 ff. in the collections made by John Donne, Jr. and Tobie Mathews, etc., the over 200 letters by Donne that have survived have much biographical and literary importance; but their style is not exceptional. I follow mostly Gosse's and Hayward's sequence, and Keynes' datings; the question of some dates and attributions is still an open question. As in group 1, here likewise are prayers by both the layman and the clergyman.

A. Hayward, #5, pp. 445 and 446, from the Loseley Ms., the beginning and ending of this long letter.

B. Hayward, #6, p. 477, from the Loseley Ms., the conclusion of this letter.

C. Tobie Mathews, p. 327, the conclusion of a very long, filial letter, exemplary in comfort. "Doctor Donne" etc. is the formal heading used by Mathews. Catholic all her life, Donne's mother eventually lived with him at St. Paul's Deanery and outlived her illustrious son.

D. Hayward, #26, pp. 476 and 478, from the Domestic State Papers of James I at the Record Office. The deletion marks indicate an extensive passage in which Donne reveals details of his manner of preaching.

E. *Letters*, #5, p. 10, and in slightly different form in Tobie Mathews, p. 108 (see Introduction, fn. 59). Bridget White who became Lady Kingsmel was long acquainted with Donne.

F. Hayward, #32, pp. 485 and 486, from the Loseley Ms. Donne had retired to the home of Sir John Danvers during the plague months of 1625. This letter is not in Gosse.

G. Hayward, #33, pp. 486 and 489, from the Domestic State Papers of James I at the Record Office. The deletion marks indicate an extensive passage. This letter's postscript tells how Donne had spent the summer in preparing the first folio of his sermons, *LXXX*, for publication.

H. *Letters*, #84, p. 233, the beginning of a long letter.

I. Tobie Mathews, pp. 348 and 349, the conclusion of the lengthy

Notes: Textual and Explanatory

"A Letter from the aforesaid Doctor Donne to the same friend, occasioned by the death of her son." See Introduction, fn. 60.

J. *Letters,* #107, p. 283, the conclusion of an average length letter.

K. *Letters,* #86, p. 241, ditto.

L. *Letters,* #110, p. 287, the conclusion of a short letter.

M. This prayer illustrates an epistle dedicatory to a printed sermon, *A sermon upon the viii Verse of the I chapter of the Acts of the Apostles.* Preach'd to the Honourable Company of the Virginian Plantation. 13° Novemb. 1622. By Iohn Donne Deane of St. Paul's, London . . . London, 1622. Sig. A 3 recto and verso. This is one of the sermons in the quarto *Three sermons upon speciall occasions* . . . 1623, *Foure sermons* . . . 1625, and *Five sermons* . . . 1626. See group 5, section G. The word *promove* means to promote, "to move on, advance, make progress" (*N.E.D.*).

GROUP 5: from the *SERMONS.* A few of Donne's sermons were printed as seperate quartos and octavos during his lifetime, 1622ff., but most were published in the folio volumes of 1640 (*LXXX*), 1649 (*Fifty*), and 1660 (*XXVI*). Indeed not all such sermons include prayers. These I have selected will indicate the preacher's system of using prayers before (as in B and C), within (as in D and A), and after (as in E to P) his sermons. Here are pulpit and public-occasion prayers, naturally more formal, yet devoutly sincere. I include a generous representation because e. g. *Donne's Sermons: Selected Passages with an Essay,* by Logan Pearsall Smith, Oxford, 1919, includes almost none.

A. *Fifty,* #26, p. 224, "Preached to the King, at White-Hall, the first Sunday in Lent," probably in 1627. This autobiographic prayer is placed first in this group to show the dominantly personal appeal Donne's sermons have.

B. *Encaenia. The Feast of Dedication.* Celebrated at Lincolne's Inne, in a Sermon there upon Ascension Day, 1623. At the Dedication of a new Chappell there, Consecrated by the Right Reverend Father in God, the Bishop of London. Preached by Iohn Donne, Deane of St. Paul's ... London 1623. Sig. A 3 recto and verso. Text: John 10, 22. Included in *Three sermons* . . . 1623, *Foure sermons* . . . 1625, and *Five sermons* . . . 1626 (see group 4, section M.)

C. *A sermon of commemoration of the Lady Dā[n]vers, late wife*

107

of S[i]r Iohn Dā[n]vers. Preach'd at Chilsey, where she was lately buried. By Iohn Donne D. of St. Paul's, Lond. 1 July 1627 ... London 1627. Sig. A 2 to A 6. Text: 2 Peter 3, 13.

D. *The first sermon preached to King Charles,* at Saint Iames: 3. April. 1625. By Iohn Donne, Deane of Saint Paul's, London . . . London 1625, pp. 5 and 6. Text: Psalm 11, 3. See Introduction, fn. 22. Included in *Foure sermons . . .* 1625, and *Five sermons . . .* 1626 (see group 4, section M).

E. *LXXX,* #14, p. 143, "Preached at White-hall, March 3. 1619," in Lent. Text: Amos 5, 18.

F. *LXXX,* #15, p. 152, "Preached at White-hall, March 8. 1621," in Lent. Text: 1 Corinthians 15, 26.

G. *A sermon upon the viii Verse of the I chapter of the Acts of the Apostles . . .* (see group 4, section M), pp. 47 to 49. In this prayer we see Donne's fondness for word play: "Heart ... heartily affected . . . heartinesse."

H. *LXXX,* #18, p. 183, "Preached at S[t]. Paul's, in the Evening, upon Easter-day. 1623." Text: Acts 2, 36 which was "Part of the second Lesson of that Evening Prayer."

I. *Encaenia . . .* (seeB), p. 41.

J. *LXXX,* #17, p. 171, "Preached at White-hall, March 4. 1624," in Lent. Text: Matthew 19, 17.

K. *LXXX,* #80 (see Introduction, fn. 2), p. 826.

L. *LXXX,* #22, p. 224, "Preached at S[t]. Paul's, upon Easter-day. 1627." Text: Hebrews 11, 35.

M. *LXXX,* #49, p. 496, "Preached on the Conversion of S[t]. Paul. 1629." Text: Acts 23, 6 and 7.

N. *LXXX,* #24, p. 241, "Preached upon Easter-day. 1629." Text: Job 4, 18.

O. *A sermon upon the xix verse of the II Chapter of Hosea . . .* 1634, in *Six sermons upon severall occasions . . .* By that late learned and reverend Divine John Donne . . . London 1634, p. 24. This is reprinted in *Fifty* as #3. As this prayer indicates, it graced a wedding ceremony.

P. *Death's Duell . . .* (see Introduction, fn. 64), Being his last Sermon, and called by his Maiestie's household The Doctor's owne Funerall Sermon . . . London 1632, p. 43. Text: Psalm 68, 20. The version in *XXVI* is slightly different in spelling and punctuation.

Notes: *Textual and Explanatory*

GROUP 6: Miscellaneous.

A. Recorded by Walton in *Life* . . . prefixed to *LXXX*, sig. B 5 recto bottom and verso top. Translated, these read:

1624 / 1625. To God all Good, all Great, the benevolent Bestower, by me and by them, for whom, by me, these sums are laid up, be glory and grace ascribed for ever. Amen.

1626. Thy mercies, O Lord, are multiplied upon us. Grant, O Lord, that what out of Thine infinite bounty Thou hast vouchsafed to lavish upon us, into whose hands it may devolve, may always be improved to thy glory. Amen.

1628. At the end of these six years remains [. . .].

1629. What have I, which I have not received from the Lord? He bestows, also, to the intent that what He hath bestowed may revert to Him by the proper use of it: that, as I have not consciously been wanting to myself during the whole course of the past year, either in discharging my secular duties, in retaining the dignity of my station, or in my conduct towards my servants and the poor—so my children for whom remains whatever is remaining, may receive it with gratitude, and acknowledge the beneficent Giver. Amen.

B. The Latin original is reprinted in *Poems,* ed. Grierson, Vol. II, p. 262. Theodorus Gaza (1398-1475) was a famous translator and teacher of Greek in the West. Among his works are numerous epistles to different persons on various literary subjects.

C. Recorded by Walton in *Life* . . . prefixed to *LXXX*, sig. B 5 recto. The details omitted between this beginning and conclusion are not printed in *LXXX*, but can be found in the amplified later editions of Walton's *Lives* . . . Doone's will was sealed December 13, 1630.